Just a

Dropped

Stitch

Just a Dropped Stitch

Laurie Levinger

An EMERALD CITY *Book*

JUST A DROPPED STITCH

Copyright © 2010 Laurie Levinger. All rights reserved. Except for brief quotations in critical publications or reviews, no part of this book may be reproduced in any manner without prior written permission from the publisher. Write: Permissions, Wipf and Stock Publishers, 199 W. 8th Ave., Suite 3, Eugene, OR 97401.

Resource Publications
An Imprint of Wipf and Stock Publishers
199 W. 8th Ave., Suite 3
Eugene, OR 97401

www.wipfandstock.com

An earlier version of "My Mother's Jewelry" appeared in *Bridges: A Jewish Feminist Journal*, Spring 2008 (c) 2008 The Bridges Association, and is reprinted with the permission of Indiana University Press.

An earlier version of "The Family Business" appeared in *Celebrating Family History: An Anthology of Prize Willing Stories*, Southern California Genealogical Society, 2005.

An earlier version of "Coach" appeared in *Absolute Write* e-zine, 2003.

The story "Blessing" originally appeared as "Blessing Impossible" in *Reform Judaism* (Fall 2003) (www.reformjudaismmag.org), published by the Union for Reform Judaism.

An earlier version of "Wife?" appeared in *Chiron Review* (Winter 2005).

An earlier version of "Next of Kin" appeared in *Out in the Mountains* (February 2004).

An earlier version of "Hiking," appeared in *Vermont Ink* (Summer 2003). It also appeared in *Austin Mama* e-zine (August 2004) as "On the Trail with Noah."

ISBN 13: 978-1-60899-067-2

Cataloging-in-Publication data:

Levinger, Laurie.

    Just a dropped stitch / Laurie Levinger.

    x + 222 p. ; 23 cm.

    ISBN 13: 978-1-60899-067-2

    1. Fiction. I. Title.

Manufactured in the U.S.A.

To my mother, Gloria,
who has been with me every step of the way,

and

To the real Noah and Sophie.
You are the lights of my life.

Contents

Acknowledgments | ix

After
1. After | 3
2. Good Night, Irene | 15
3. My Mother's Jewelry | 19

Dropped Stitch
4. Dropped Stitch | 35

Family Business
5. The Family Business | 43
6. Naming Ourselves | 49
7. Learning to Swim | 54

The Little Girl
8. Bezel | 59
9. Ice | 63
10. The Grocery Store | 67

Hard Listening
11. What I Heard | 75
12. Fire | 83

Right Work
13. Vincent | 91
14. Looking for Work | 97
15. The Tiger's Eye | 99
16. Coach | 105
17. 6 Hens and a Robin | 111
18. Getting the Mail | 115

Too Big

19 Too Big | 121
20 Binky | 124

Telling

21 The Letter | 131
22 The Hero | 139
23 Like Air | 153
24 Wife? | 159
25 Next of Kin | 172
26 Blessing | 175

Sophie

27 The Dress | 185
28 On the Bridge, Twice | 190

Noah

29 Hiking | 197
30 Dear John | 204

Love Made Visible

31 Characters | 209
32 Thanks to Itzhak | 212
33 Chinese Box | 217

Afterword | 221

Acknowledgments

MY THANKS TO:

Dina Yellen, the real Dorothy, who introduced me to a new way of listening and told me to write;

Ulrike Guthrie, my editor and agent, who had faith in this manuscript and brought it out of the drawer where it was languishing;

K. C. Hanson and the people at Wipf and Stock who turned the manuscript into a book.

Ellen Lesser, my writing coach, who tolerated my idiosyncratic use of punctuation and helped me find my voice;

The Women's Group, chosen sisters, friends for life; and

My family, who supported me even when it wasn't easy.

After

1

After

"I NEVER THOUGHT I'D LIVE to see sixty," my mother said, gripping the side of the wood tub, skin stretched thin over her knuckles as she lowered her body tenderly, inch by tentative inch, into the steaming water. We all looked away into the dark night as her enormous breast, threatening to escape the confines of her suit, floated on the surface before disappearing into bubbles. We were a crowd that night, our modest family in bathing suits, soaking together in the hot tub: my father in his usual place beside my mother, my big brother Ben, me with my lover Ruth pressed close to me, then Isaac, the youngest. Plus spouses or soon-to-be ex-spouses. The circle was complete, or almost. Because our middle brother, Jon, was on-his-way, be-there-soon.

"I just didn't believe I'd be here to celebrate this day," she repeated, forcing us at least to nod, mutely. This evening, just the way she wanted it: water, warmth, togetherness. We each pretended a smile, looking into her eyes, easier now that the breast was gone, below the waterline.

But six months later the crowd had thinned and it was just my father and I taking care of my mother during her dying. There are so many things I could tell you about what happened in our family, but maybe I should begin by describing what my life was like *before* we understood how sick she really was, during that time we didn't call it dying, even to ourselves.

For you to fully enter into this story and to understand my state of mind, I'd have to tell you about the end of my relationship with Ruth. We'd been together since college and, now bumping up against middle age, after years of endless discussion, we'd finally decided to have a child. That longed-for baby, Noah, was now a toddler who took up more space than anyone only two feet tall had any right to. Noah centered us, transforming us into mothers, as well as the lovers we'd been for more than ten years. And yet, in those last moments when everything could've been perfect—a renovated farmhouse, a loving relationship, our new baby—before my mother was obviously dying, somehow it wasn't. The month before we learned that she wasn't going to get better, my world tilted on an unimagined axis when Ruth told me, "Noah's everything I've ever dreamed of, he fulfills a need I didn't know I had, but something's still missing, I don't know what." She needed more space (*from me*, is what I heard) to sort it out. She moved from our home in New Canaan village, leaving me alone with Noah.

We shared custody, but like all beloved children Noah had full-time residence in my head. Which had everything to do with how I felt driving over the mountains to visit my mother every weekend. Alone in the car, I ricocheted between rage and longing as I drove the four hours from my empty house to my mother's home in Albany, where I arrived buffeted, limp with exhaustion, dreading what I'd find. And then when it was time to go, I'd leave her house dreading what was waiting for me when I got back home. It didn't matter to my exuberant toddler how many memories crowded in on me, demanding attention. In his mind he came first. It didn't matter how empty the house felt. Reality stared me down: I was single again, a mother myself, even while I witnessed my mother dying, weekend by weekend.

But let me take a minute away from the emptiness of my house in Vermont to introduce you to my three brothers who had been (or should have been) in the hot tub that night: Ben, Jon and Isaac. Ben, The Perfect Oldest Son: smart, handsome, responsible. Four years later I came along. Jon came so close after me that we were almost twins, but we grew up as different as two people can be. He was The Brilliant One, socially awkward, the child most like our father. Then, Isaac, the baby. Arriving ten years after Jon, everyone assumed he was *a mistake* but my mother confronted the unspoken question directly by proclaiming, "We planned each of our babies." Isaac was The Talented One, considered a musical prodigy by his tone-deaf family. Listening to classical music records before he was two, he could identify each by the color of the label. "That's Beethoven, that's Bach," he'd say when we showed him off to our friends. *See, I told you he could do it. Isn't that amazing?*

I occupied a unique spot, too. I was The Girl.

We all looked alike—variations on a theme—so there wasn't any point in trying to deny family ties. For years I'd be somewhere I thought no one in the family could possibly have gone before me, when someone would demand, knowing the answer, "Aren't you Ben's (Jon's, Isaac's) sister?" But obviously, looking the same isn't the same as *being* the same, and we each brought our own story to our mother's dying, a direct result of how we felt about her when she was still giving us all "a piece of her mind" and "running the show." She was always saying things like that—clichés really—but delivered with such certainty that there was no disputing her.

No question that if my brothers were here they'd have plenty to say—corrections and complaints (*that's not how I felt, that's not what happened*)—about how I'm telling this story. But this is my version.

Ben and Isaac had each come to visit before those last days. I'm not sure whether they knew enough to really say goodbye, and since no one talked about it, there was no way to tell for certain. We were a family that had always been praised for how we confronted difficulties—how we could talk about *everything*—how close we were, in spite of our differences. We'd bought the public perception, but when it came to the most intimate moments, like saying goodbye, it was *"every man for himself."* (Another one of my mother's favorite sayings. I always wondered if that included her and me, but it was too late to ask.)

There were lots of visitors coming in and out of the house, but by that last weekend, everyone who was going to come had come already, and now it was just my father and I taking care of my mother.

We could tell she was getting sick, I mean *really* sick, when she put her knitting down. She'd already stopped going to yarn shops—"What do you think, mohair or alpaca this time, Jesse?"—stopped picking out patterns for the sweaters, vests, stocking caps and socks she gave us all at Christmas. Even after I'd stopped celebrating Christmas, something knitted would arrive, wrapped in red paper with bright green trees. When she set her needles and yarn neatly on her bedside table, the music of clacking needles quieted, her hands finally still, that stilling was a preview of what was to come. "I'll pick it up when my energy comes back," as she turned away in bed.

I could describe my mother's room, how it started to smell because we didn't know that she'd need a catheterization bag. How the light came gently through the fake-lace curtains that filtered the winter sun, making it even weaker. That my father slept in the bed beside her until the day before. When the stench of urine got so suffocating that it was impossible to think of anything else, I suggested he sleep on the living room couch. But he refused. I—at least—could not tell him what to do. The last coherent sentence I heard my mother say was, "Curl around me, Joe"—request and command rolled into one. I was staying upstairs in my old bedroom where I hadn't slept since high school, which might have snapped me back towards my angry adolescent self if circumstances had been different. As it was, I wandered through the night, up and down the stairs, checking on them. The mattress we'd dragged beside the bed was unoccupied. My father had fallen asleep next to my mother in his usual place. She was asleep or unconscious, I couldn't tell. Her cat, Satchmo, stayed curled against her, like a comma, until the very end.

Those last couple of days my mother didn't say much and most of what she did say seemed to come from that other world she was moving into. So when she called out Jon's name, I didn't understand. My father and I were there—*was she calling us?* Ben and Isaac had both visited. Jon was somewhere else, wrestling with his ambivalence. He was the one person she called for before she stopped calling out at all.

I could pull a different thread, unraveling the story from a different place: What she said before she stopped talking. Or I could try to describe the color of Ben's face when he emerged from our mother's room the last night of his visit. I'd been waiting up for him, leaning against the wall outside the bedroom. He stayed with her so long I was considering leaving my post. Then he came out, looking like he'd seen a ghost. People say that all the time, you know, but I never thought I'd hear myself say it. It's the truth, though. His face was changed, lines of humor and tenderness gone; all the bursting vitality that made him so charismatic wiped away. A blank mask, eyes looking inward at something no one else could see. And he was a color I don't think there's a word for. "Ben," calling him quietly. He looked toward the sound, unfocused, as he slid into the faded green chair by the telephone stand, dropping his head into his hands. "Ben, what is it? You look terrible."

"Nothing. I can't say."

I put my arm around him and he half-turned to me. "She asked me—" stopping, his breath staccato. "I can't tell you."

"Ben, you have to. I'm the one who's taking care of her. You have to tell me."

"I can't."

"Ben?"

"She asked me to kill her."

Kill her?

What do I do now? Do I stay with my haunted big brother? Or go to my dying mother who's trying to get someone to help her choreograph her own exit?

"What did you say?" *Do I want to know this?*

"No. I told her I wanted to help. But I couldn't do that. I told her . . . I said I was sorry, but that I couldn't do it." He looked at me then, full-face, and there in his deep brown eyes I caught a glimpse of what he'd seen. "I've never said that to her before." Quickly turning away, he said, "I'm going out for a walk. Don't come, Jesse" closing the door gently behind him.

You know how in every crisis you can look back and it seems like there's a line where you cross over and everything changes; there's a *before* and an *after*? I learned this one day years before when I was out for a drive with a friend—no particular destination, we weren't driving to learn anything important, but as we passed a swamp, she pointed out the window. "This is where the water changes direction. After here the rivers run north." Just like that.

In our case the dividing line was some*one*, not something. My father and I were worried, not sure if we were doing enough to take care of my mother. He'd always hated talking on the phone but I urged him to call the doctor. He refused, "I don't want to bother him," but I persisted. Finally he gave in and did, I heard him in his measured voice, describing her unmoving, heavy body. This young doctor wasn't used to making house calls, something that had gone out of style long before he was born. But he came anyway, stopping on his way home from work. He stepped into the bedroom, took one look, and motioned us out. Standing in the hall, not wasting words—he was late for dinner after all—he said, "It's time to get hospice in here."

My father was never much for words. I, on the other hand, took after my mother and almost always have something to say. But not then. We nodded, silent accomplices.

The someone who divided our before from our after was Simon, the hospice nurse, a wiry, quiet man I felt, somehow, I'd known before. Maybe his being gay was part of what made him so familiar, I don't know. I just knew he felt almost like one of my real brothers.

Simon asked my father and me each to tell him about his new patient. My father went first. When it was my turn, proud of my knowledge of her medical history, I reeled off dates, diagnoses, remissions, and metastasis. Simon listened like he had all the time in the world. When I'd finished my presentation he reached over to touch my shoulder and said softly, "I'm here now. It's time for you to just be her daughter." That made all the difference in the world.

But I should double back again and fill you in on what happened before Simon came that made the after so distinctly different.

My father and I had agreed to take care of my mother at home, since that's what she wanted. We'd been trying to keep her comfortable. After she stopped talking and couldn't tell us if she was hungry, we had to guess when she might want to eat. Food had been a major topic of conversation at our house and we just knew that she wouldn't be excited about what we offered. But we braved her disapproval, even when she scowled, disgusted, at the mushed food. She bit at the spoon half full of applesauce, a primitive reflex or anger, who could tell? One evening at what should have been dinnertime I watched my father feed her sips of water with a baby spoon. When he finished he announced proudly that she'd drunk at least an ounce. That's how we measured success. Later I realized her nightgown was damp. She'd dribbled it down her front. I changed her without telling him why.

Two days later, just before dawn, I went downstairs to their bedroom. Something was different, even the air had changed. Then I knew: this was the day my mother would die.

Simon had been with us for two days now, but his shift didn't start until seven, so my father and I had to turn my mother over. We'd been doing this once a day, until Simon told we should do it more often, because of bedsores. I had years of experience working in hospitals, so I'd seen a lot, but I was a medical social worker, I'd never actually given hands-on care, except to sit on a patient's bed and hold a hand, talking. These last several weeks I'd welcomed the opportunity to try to *do* something. I wanted to touch my mother, to make her comfortable, to do a good job. Whatever it took. But as we learned what taking care of her was all about, I recognized again that talking was what I did best.

So along with turning her and changing the sheets and her nightgown, I was talking, always talking to her, remembering what my colleagues had told me, that hearing is the last thing to go, that people can hear even when they can't answer. So I told her all sorts of things about what was going on: "Mom, Heidi came to see you today. She said the other women in your group send their love. Rachel and Dottie are planning to come tomorrow. And, you know who called? Herman. He's in France, but he'll be home next week, and said he'd come see you. And, let's see, Isaac is dating a new girl, her name is Kathy, she's a physical therapist. Oh, and I talked to Ruth who said Noah's learned some new words, he can say 'Mommy's at Grammy's'. Isn't that great?" When I ran out of news I said, "I love you."

I love you. "I love you."

My father and I had an unspoken pact that even we didn't realize we'd made: keeping my mother's body clear and unbroken meant we could prevent the inevitable. We conspired to outwit death.

Even though we knew about bedsores, when my father and I turned her over that Tuesday morning and saw them, I wasn't prepared for red ulcerations oozing, weeping, on my mother's hips, elbows and shoulders. I couldn't have imagined what bedsores would look like on a body I loved.

Those bedsores were an assault on our commitment and our competence.

I felt sick waiting for Simon. I knew he would pull back the blankets and uncover our failure. As if it were about success or failure, or about us at all, instead of about her. But since Simon was a real nurse and had seen his share of bedsores, he wasn't shocked. He looked closely at her, and then turned to us. "She's not in pain. That's just what happens when the body breaks down." And then, knowing that we needed reassuring, "You didn't do anything wrong."

Relieved, my father decided he'd go to the grocery store. He hadn't left the house in days, so when he didn't come back for a while I didn't worry. Just pleased he'd decided to take some time for himself. When he finally did get home, he explained, "I turned left out of the driveway and drove 'full speed ahead in the wrong direction,' as Gloria says." He had lived in that house for twenty-five years and he'd gotten lost on his way to the store.

This is what I'm trying to tell you: that we didn't know what we were doing, but we learned on the job. That we needed help and reassurance, and Simon—who did know what he was doing—offered it. We didn't believe anything would make a difference if it didn't take us back to before my mother was dying. But we were wrong. When it came close enough to touch us on the shoulder, we accepted help.

And that even though we were staring the inevitable straight in the face, we weren't able to speak its name. We believed that saying the word would somehow, magically, make it real. So we didn't say it.

What *is* real is the way that my mother died. At a time when it would be natural for her to lash out or to retreat inward, away from the demands of a noisy world, my mother was still herself. Until she drifted off into that world of half-life, she stayed the same, talking, looking out, focusing on other people.

One morning when she was still able to talk, I got a call from my therapist and, needing privacy, I stretched the long phone cord to its limit into the kitchen. There, sitting at the kitchen table—my mother's domain—I cried, because I'd never sit there with her again discussing problems, asking her advice. I let myself say the unthinkable aloud to someone outside the family. "How much longer can she survive like this?"

After, I stopped in the bathroom to pull myself together—that's how we say it in my family—before I went back to her room. She turned slowly towards me, "Sweetie, what's wrong?" That did it. No soft tears dripping down my cheeks for me, I erupted in sobs. I'd always counted on her empathy, but at a time like this I felt selfish wanting it. I sank to the floor, leaning my head on her bed. "Poor Sweetie Pie, you're losing your Mommy," she murmured as she stroked my hair. Saying *Mommy*—I hadn't called her that for years—and calling me by my baby name: that was what unraveled me. When I finally got a hold of myself, I said, "But, Mom, you're losing your *life*." I climbed on the bed, putting my arm around her, curling up like we'd spent a lifetime sleeping that way. Sniffling, we cried ourselves to sleep.

Was that before or after we planned her funeral? She'd been giving me such a jumble of instructions—"I want this, no, that's not right, this is how you should do it"—I knew I'd never remember everything. So I said, "Mom, wait, let me get something to write on." I wrote down everything just the way she told me. (I still have that pad somewhere. The faded yellow page with brave handwritten notes reminds me of the daughter I was, trying to do just what my mother wanted.)

My mother was Jewish, but she'd never had any affection for the religion she'd been born into. She always told us, "My parents were hypocrites about religion. They went to Temple just to be seen and to parade around in their finery. My father wanted to show off his family to his cronies. I didn't want any part of that." But she hadn't just left Judaism quietly behind in her past. She'd disdained organized religion her whole life bringing us up with progressive causes that were supposed to take its place. Later on, she joined the Quakers, which seemed strange to me given their silent worship—*how could she sit there without making commentary?*—but maybe it was a relief to her to *have to* be quiet. Anyway, she became an active Quaker, attending countless potlucks and political meetings, organizing a day care center in the low-income housing project where she worked with friends from her Quaker meeting. She was a natural bridge.

After my mother died, we had a family meeting about how to honor her. Deciding to have a memorial service was easy, but what about *shiva*? Some of us had begun to take tentative, baby steps to reclaim our Jewishness and we proposed visiting hours at my father's house. We couldn't quite bring ourselves to *call* it "sitting *shiva*."

We didn't know what we were getting into, but we agreed to try. So it came as a shock that *shiva* was, in fact, meaningful, that sitting around telling stories, looking at old photographs and laughing: this was a ritual that helped. Remembering that her favorite song was "Somewhere Over the Rainbow," that when she was young, people used to tell her she looked like Judy Garland. I found a photograph recently of the young Judy Garland and it was true, they did look surprisingly alike. All her life my mother worried about being overweight—even when she wasn't—so looking like Judy Garland must have really *been* something.

You know how sometimes a funeral is so orchestrated that all the uniqueness of the individual, who that person really was, disappears behind formalities? Not my mother's memorial service. It was just like her: unstructured, quirky, full of stories. I told about how she and I decided where contributions should be sent. She'd been insistent that money go to the Quakers. Trying to be helpful, I kept suggesting charities that I thought she should consider, saying things like, "Well, that's great, Mom, but what about Albany Medical Center?" or, "That's a good idea, but how about the Visiting Nurses Association?" She'd been a Visiting Nurse before she was diagnosed with breast cancer.

"No," she insisted, her gravelly voice even deeper than usual. "The QUAKERS."

So the Quakers it was. Everyone laughed when I finished. It was so like my mother. Definitive, nothing subtle. And like me, too, always making suggestions, exploring all the options, just one more thing to consider. But as usual, she got her way in the end.

I said, "So many people here today have said that my mother made them feel special. But I *know* I was special."

That was her gift to each of us. It would last a lifetime.

1987. One of the coldest Januarys on record. It was so frigid all through that endless winter only a backhoe could have broken into frozen ground. My father refused to spend extra money for a winter grave. The burial would have to wait.

We were suspended. It was a time between.

Then, suddenly it seemed, the ground thawed. I wrote a poem, driving over the mountains one last time, this time to bury my mother.

> You are
>
> Beyond words,
>
> Like a baby
>
> Before quickening.
>
> Silent
>
> presence.
>
> Still life
>
> Curled inside me.
>
> Quiet guide.

We all traveled from our separate homes to my father's house. Even Ruth and Simon came. We walked to the cemetery together and gathered around my mother's coffin. Simon stood in the circle between my father and me. We held hands. We sang "Somewhere Over the Rainbow." Someone told a story. We laughed.

Then we all went our separate ways.
To a lifetime of afters.

2

Good Night, Irene

"She's gone, Dad," I told my father. He jerked his head up, startled awake from a half-doze. Glassy-eyed, staring at me like I'd said something unthinkable. Obscene. Like we hadn't been sitting at her bedside, waiting, listening to her struggle to breathe, an eternity between inhalations. How could anyone breathe so little, live so long? Hoping she'd inhale again, praying she wouldn't.

We'd been listening to those ragged breaths, that unmistakable death-rattle. "Death-rattle," I'd always considered that an overblown, dramatic phrase used to describe some young soldier dying on a battlefield in ages gone by. But once you've heard that sound, you know it's not reserved for young boys caught off-guard by death. It's not that particular, that picky. This raspy breathing, rattling deep in the throat, the interminable pausing between, this belonged to my mother's last night.

I'd stepped out of her bedroom to answer the phone, talked fast to get back to my post by the bed. My father was sitting there too, on the other side. We'd spent the day like that, the three of us. Breathless. Waiting. So it shouldn't have come as a surprise when it came, exactly what we'd been waiting for.

"She's gone."

It was obvious. A new quiet filled her room, the air a different texture from the excruciating stillness-between-breaths we'd witnessed all day.

He stared at me, eyes calling me a liar, and then leaping to his feet, stumbled into the bathroom. "Where's a mirror?" he shouted. "I need a mirror, I've got to see if she's breathing."

It had felt like just the three of us, but really there were other people there that night. My mother's friends, Mohammed and Dina, and Ben's wife, Claudia, had come to take me out to dinner. It was my thirty-seventh birthday, and they insisted it would be good for me to leave the house. I refused, stubbornly retreating to my mother's bedside. *I don't give a damn about my birthday. I don't care what's good for me, I won't go.* The doorbell rang later, interrupting the silence. A man delivering Chinese take-out stood at the door, a bill in his outstretched hand. White cartons sat untouched, slowly cooling on the dining room table, as we all went back to our posts.

There were the phone calls. I called Simon first, who told me who to call next: the medical examiner would come to declare her dead, the funeral home men would come to remove the body. Already a new status, a shift in language—*the body*—not a person with a name who could demand things, speak for herself.

Then Claudia took over, calling family: first Ben, then Jon, and Isaac. She'd just put down the receiver when the phone—which seemed to have taken on a life of its own—rang. Thank God Claudia answered and not me, because it was Grandma Crystal, my mother's mother. Always clever with words, Claudia talked to the old woman, the mother whose daughter had just died, explaining gently that she couldn't talk to her Gloria. "She's resting comfortably," Claudia told my grandmother, and it wasn't a lie.

Grandma Crystal was too old to travel, and hadn't made it up to visit. We'd all conspired to keep the truth from her, so she couldn't have known how close the end was. How did she know to call right at that exact moment, the first time the phone was free, five minutes after her child had died? They'd never even been close.

My father was sitting beside the bed, staring at my mother as she stiffened. Smaller somehow. Lost. Kneeling on the floor next to him, I patted his hand, murmuring his name, until I realized there was something even more important for me to do. Something only I could.

Dress my mother.

She had never been vain exactly, but she did care how she looked. Once she got cancer, she had more important things to concentrate on than trying whatever the newest diet was, and she gave up struggling to lose weight. But she felt that her body had betrayed her in some essential way, and *looking pretty* took on added significance. And so when she showed me the last dress she'd bought for herself, chosen when she was still going to craft fairs and picking out exquisite handmade things, I knew I was looking at it, her final outfit.

"Isn't it lovely?" she said, telling me to hold the dress up. And it was.

A deep green corduroy for warmth, with intricate embroidery in reds, blues, and purples at the neck and sleeves. It had a gently scooped neckline perfect for showing a dying woman's best features, her lively eyes and generous face. Everything else hidden by the voluptuous folds of the billowing skirt.

I got the dress from her closet, laying it gently over a chair. I went through her jewelry box and picked out the long chain that looked like woven gold she'd bought in Mexico when my brothers and I were kids; an ancient memory flashed by from years of admiring her when she'd get dressed up, wearing that necklace, when she went out with my father.

And then I made the mistake that is so stupid I can't begin to remember what I was thinking—because obviously I wasn't. Even though it's a mistake that makes absolutely no difference. Bowing to some conventional notion of propriety, I picked out stockings for my mother to be buried in. All her life she hated stockings and wore knee socks whenever she could get away with it and still look half-way respectable.

Then the knock, and the funeral men arrived. Muscular and silent, they walked into the room, staring straight ahead, waiting for direction. Intent on doing a job. The funeral director, dressed in a somber black suit, tiny in comparison, flitted around the edges of the room, murmuring condolences.

After everything we'd seen, everything we'd done to take care of her, now someone else was in charge. The funeral director asked us to leave the room. And we did. What did he think we would see that we hadn't already seen a hundred times before? But we didn't protest, we just ceded to his authority and stepped out into the hall, obedient sentinels.

When the men shuffled out of her bedroom they were weighted down, carrying an enormous bundle wrapped in black plastic. It zipped up the sides like a garment bag you take on airplanes. The body. I nearly shrieked, "Don't turn her upside down like that, she gets dizzy!" when they twisted around the corner, angling her out the back door. Into the cold of the deepest January night.

A wall of frigid air slammed me as I followed my mother out to the hearse. The stars seemed even closer and brighter than usual. Fellow witnesses.

Frozen in that penetrating night, breath turned to ice in my throat. I started to sing. I hadn't planned to; I hardly recognized my own voice. But it didn't seem right to say goodbye without doing something.

> *Irene, good night, Irene, good night,*
> *Good night, Irene, good night, Irene.*
> *I'll see you in my dreams.*

As I sent her off, stockings and all.

3

My Mother's Jewelry

The first time I saw Reggie Newcomb I had no idea how important he'd become in my life. He's just not someone I ever would've met, or had the occasion to think much about, if we hadn't moved next door to him. I was out mowing the grass—*my very own lawn*—a couple of weeks after we'd moved into our new house, and there was Reggie, a tall, heavy man, sporting a military haircut, sweating as he carefully mowed overlapping swaths on his tiny front lawn. I waved, my best imitation of friendly-but-not-intrusive Vermont greeting. He gestured back in my direction—hard to decipher if it was neighborly or dismissive—but, *let's be optimistic and assume he's just shy*, as I maneuvered my mower to the patch of grass closest to his. Reggie pushed his mower parallel to mine, but since he didn't turn his off, I didn't either, so we shouted our hellos. He smiled, one of those smiles where the lips pull back showing teeth, but the eyes never change. I could see Reggie Newcomb wasn't happy to have Ruth and me for his new neighbors.

When we'd moved into the little farmhouse on Romance Lane, in the pristine countryside surrounding New Canaan village, we thought we'd finally arrived at a place where we could stay put. The village was a visual cliché, straight out of an old edition of *Vermont Life*, and even the name of the dirt road promised us a future of happiness. The morning we saw the house it was just a shell, but I could tell it would be home. Ruth and I were good at making decisions quickly, at least when it came to houses. We made an offer that afternoon and immediately started talking to the builder about knocking down walls, putting up others, and screening in the back porch. We could already see ourselves sleeping out there on hot summer nights, Noah in his little crib beside our antique brass bed, the three of us listening to the animals rustling and the stream murmuring as we drifted off to sleep.

It was a wonderful space.

Ruth and I had already lived together for ten years in Madison and when it was time to leave there our plan was to head west to Oregon, a PhD program for her, a social work job for me. I'd support her while she finished her degree and then we'd take the next step whatever that might be. But then we got the news that my mother had cancer; we reversed direction, and moved to Boston to be close by. Ruth finagled a last minute admission to graduate school, and I found a job as a hospital administrator.

Life in Boston was full of work and new friends. We were near enough to visit my parents often, and far enough away to maintain our privacy. My mother had surgery, then a year of chemotherapy. Her cancer went into remission.

Everything should have been fine, although tinged with the uncertainty of my mother's cancer. But something was still missing. Finally, after months and months of endless processing, listening, disagreeing, negotiating—this wasn't something you could compromise about—Ruth finally agreed that the time was right for us to start a family. It took almost a year of trying, but finally I got pregnant. Ruth had just finished her degree, and when she was offered her first faculty position at a small college in northern Vermont the timing seemed perfect. We could see our future together: I'd quit my job and we'd move north, the baby would be born in Vermont, I'd stay home for several months, and then find work. I wasn't really concerned about whether that work was in my field or not. At this stage I was more excited about being a new mother than about my career, anyway.

So, we rented out our house in Boston and moved north. That first year we lived in a two hundred-year-old farmhouse to experience what it was like living in the country. After the noise of city life I relished the silence, the isolation, and being surrounded by fields where cows grazed. I never felt lonely because it turned out that I was one of those women who love being pregnant, feeling beautiful and serene as I got bigger. Bigger. Huge. Ruth took to calling me "Beachy" (as in beached whale) when we discovered that I could not turn over in bed without her help. I decided that this was funny, a friendly nickname.

Our new lifestyle was so peaceful it was easy to imagine raising our child in the country. Which is why we decided it was time to cut ties by selling our house in the city, and buying one in Vermont. Noah was born in April and we moved into our newly renovated farmhouse two months later.

The house on Romance Lane was ideal for a new mother. The dirt road meandered a mile up and down hills, crossing a waterfall before arriving at the general store, the village heart. Every morning I pushed Noah in his stroller to the store, bought a snack, then pushed him home, singing the spirituals my mother had sung to me when I was a baby. After our walk we'd both be hungry again, so we'd eat lunch, and take naps. Later I planted flowering perennials while he watched, beatific in his bouncy chair.

My new life: too perfect to be real. We were living in a postcard-town, where tourists came to vacation. Our baby was easy and beautiful. Everything had fallen into place. I belonged right here. After a lifetime of moving, I'd finally come home.

The only minor distraction was Reggie. Other neighbors had dropped over to welcome us, and oohed and aahed over Noah. The town postmistress who lived across the road knew everything about everyone in town. While we ate the homemade blueberry cake she brought over, she filled us in about our neighbor: Reggie was a fundamentalist minister who'd started a private school for local children. "He doesn't trust the local school will teach Christian values," the postmistress told us.

This didn't bode well. I'd lived here long enough to know that while the Yankee attitude of good-fences-make-good-neighbors might guarantee that Reggie wouldn't confront us directly, small-town gossip would ensure that he'd know a different kind of family was living right next door.

Which was true, but even so, it turned out that Reggie wasn't my main problem. Because within six months everything had changed.

I've told you that Ruth decided something was wrong with her life, and that she needed to live alone to sort things out. This translated to her leaving our home on Romance Lane to move even further north, almost to the Canadian border. I loved her enough to try to give her the time she said she needed to sort out her feelings, even though what I felt was that she couldn't quite bring herself to tell me it was over, that I was being left for good. She moved out in early October when tourists flock to our part of Vermont. My life turned away from postcard-perfect fall. While leaf-peepers arrived by the bus load to enjoy the crisp air, to marvel at the miraculous color—snapping photos, "Hey, Nancy, look at that tree! How about that color!"—all I could see was leaves dying around me.

It was then, a couple of weeks after Ruth left, that I got the news my mother wouldn't live with breast cancer much longer. But regardless of dying leaves and my dying mother, Ruth and I had to keep seeing each other. We'd agreed, while I was trying to get pregnant, even before there was a real Noah, that if we were lucky enough to have a baby, we would *both* always be our baby's parents. So this became my new reality: shared custody, juggling schedules and making arrangements to meet halfway to exchange our toddler.

Ruth got her space. I got the house on Romance Lane.

My mother never got to see it, though. I'd told her all about the house, and she'd even made helpful suggestions for the renovation. But when I could have really used a visit, she was too exhausted to travel. Sometimes I would take Noah when I went to see her on weekends, thinking he'd be a good distraction, maybe make her laugh. But usually I left him with Ruth, and drove over the mountains to visit her alone. In the beginning, I talked about Ruth and how I'd always thought we'd be one of those couples who works things out and stays together, *maybe this is just a bump in the road?* My mother listened sympathetically, and gave me good advice like she always had. We dispensed with our old rule from my teenage years that she was allowed to offer her opinion only if I asked for it. Now I just paid attention to whatever she had to say, glad she could talk to me at all. But as she got weaker she didn't seem to want to hear about my problems with Ruth. Sometimes she talked about being sick, and once—just once—she broached the topic of dying. That day she asked me to help her plan her funeral, and I did. But mostly she was interested in the family: how my brothers were, what their kids were up to, what was going on with Noah. She'd loved Ruth for more than ten years but she didn't ask about her anymore. She only had energy for the people closest to her.

One long, dark afternoon a week or so before my mother died, she told me to bring her jewelry box to her. I placed it gently on her lap and opened the top for her, and was nearly swept away by the sudden undertow of memories, because, there laid out in the box was every piece of jewelry she'd ever owned. Some beautiful and unique, gifts to her from my father's foreign students. It must be a sign of respect for students to give the professor's wife a special present, because she sure had a lot of them: the necklace with tiny ivory elephants from India, jade from Guatemala, inlaid glass beads from Florence. Some of the pieces were nostalgic: silver earrings from the year we lived in Mexico, a JFK button, her Phi Beta Kappa key, and the graduation pin from nursing school (at forty-four she was the oldest new nurse, and the only one whose kids came to the ceremony). Some of the rest was cheap and gaudy; I had no idea where those pieces came from or what they meant to her. True to form, she treasured each one whether or not it was "good." I'd always teased her saying that her taste ran from the sublime to the ridiculous.

I offered that familiar joke again, as she picked through the box slowly— she'd begun to do everything slowly by then—examining each piece like she was trying to understand it. "Jesse, I want you to have these," handing me a gold band with the tiny emerald Ben had brought home from Colombia the summer he tutored English, the blue brooch that had been my grandmother's, the delicate necklace with the string of miniature ivory elephants. She cupped them in her hand for a long minute, feeling their weight, remembering, before she held them out to me. "I loved these, and I'd love for you to have them."

After my mother died, when the memorial service and the *shiva* were over, I went back to my house in New Canaan. Ruth had been taking care of Noah, and she brought him home to me. I struggled to yank my life back on track for Noah's sake. But there wasn't anything familiar to anchor me to this new version of reality. I tried in as many ways as I could to console myself: I cried a lot, I called friends in the middle of the night. I created a mini-shrine out of some photographs and the jewelry my mother had given me, setting it up on my bedroom bureau where I'd see it first thing every morning.

And I went back to work. I found daycare for Noah and opened my own private therapy practice. I worked part-time so I could still spend lots of time with Noah, but work filled some essential need. Focusing on other people's problems was demanding and required me to take a break from my own, which helped me to contain crippling grief. Whatever form it might take, whether a tsunami or tornado, the result would be the same. I would be swept away. No time for minor problems, survival was my priority. *What I need is a barricade to survive behind. I need a suit of full body armor.*

In such a perilous situation, living next to Reggie disappeared as a problem. In fact, when I remembered it at all, it made me nostalgic for my former life when I'd been able to consider him a concern worth worrying about.

Several months after my mother died, Reggie and I had our second conversation. I'd put my old VW up for sale and he came across the driveway to look at it; he was shopping for a car for his teenage son, who had a well-deserved reputation as the village hot-rodder—*boy, I wonder what old Reggie makes of that?*—but that was hardly my business. After a brief discussion we made a deal. All very reasonable and neighborly.

Then I packed Noah up and left town to visit friends for the weekend. When I got home on Sunday afternoon, I realized I'd forgotten to give Reggie the title to the car, which I'd promised to do. There he was in his garden, squatting, weeding. He listened to my apology, eyes glazed over, then nodding he said, "That's okay, I have the title."

"You have the title? But how did you get it?"

"I have it. The Lord led me to it."

I just stood there. Speechless. Blank. *Where did I leave the title? Wasn't it in my desk drawer?* I just stood there, having sprouted roots. Blinking. Then I spun away, pushing through the hydrangea bushes that separated our yards, and stumbled up the steps into my own house.

Usually I would've called a friend to laugh about something so absurd or to ask if they thought this was serious, but this time I decided I'd better not mention it to anyone. Absurd or terrifying— just too bizarre—I didn't want my friends worrying about me living next to a person who would do something like that. *Thank God I decided to be wary of the guy. Obviously the best stance with Reggie is to be polite, but distant. I certainly don't want to make someone like him mad. God, who knows what he might do next!* I just kept shaking my head, trying to amuse myself with jokes about the Lord's many abilities.

But the next morning, while I was still trying to figure out whether this was psychotic and scary, or absurdly funny, everything shifted again. Because I felt so off-center, it dawned on me that this would be a perfect day to wear my mother's jewelry. Like an amulet. I went to the mini-shrine to choose just the right piece to help stabilize me. But something was different. Looking carefully, it was obvious: *why hadn't I noticed before?* The blue brooch and the gold ring were missing.

Don't panic, maybe the cat knocked them down. I dropped to my hands and knees and swept my arm under the bureau, hunting frantically. Nothing. Just dust.

This time I wasn't speechless. I knew exactly what to do. I called the police to report the theft. An officer arrived at my house within minutes. He was young, serious in his carefully pressed uniform and spit-shined black shoes. "You might not believe this," I said, "but my neighbor just told me that the Lord led him into my house to get the car title." Obviously intrigued, he didn't miss a beat as he assured me, "We've got our man."

But they didn't. In spite of whatever investigation that enthusiastic new officer conducted, they never did find my mother's jewelry.

I had to make space in my life to live with my losses: the loss of that profound sense of safety because I lived in what I believed to be a bucolic haven, safe from the problems of the big city. Reality intruded, and I discovered that my closest neighbor was a man whose God gave him divine permission to break into other people's homes.

I'd never wear my mother's jewelry again, or be able to ask her advice. She'd been my confidante, the person I enjoyed unscripted conversation with, the person I brought my joy, like carrying a gift, stories of Noah's many antics. Even when she was so sick she could barely think, she'd remember to ask me, "What color socks is he wearing today?" Important things like that. She never hung up the phone without saying, "I love you, and Noah, too, Sweetie Pie." There were so many problems we would have dissected and solved together.

But I coped. One of my strategies was to immerse myself in Buddhism. I learned to meditate, coming to understand that my attachment to the jewelry was the source of my pain. I could hold on to memories of my mother. They were what was important.

In my mind I built a box, as impenetrable as a fireproof lock box, that contained all my feelings, and that helped. So did time. I reminded myself whenever I got mad all over again, *you can't live in fear and anger, it's over and done with, for god's sake, just let it go.* And mostly I was able to put it behind me where it belonged.

That would have been the end of the story, except one morning several years after I'd left Romance Lane behind, my eye caught a newspaper headline. What was past came crashing into the present. Because there was my old neighbor Reggie, making news.

NEW CANAAN CHAPLAIN CHARGED
IN CRIMES AGAINST CHILDREN

What? What's this all about? I began reading:

> ... five counts of lewd and lascivious contacts of a sexual nature occurring over a decade ... People in town knew something was happening with Newcomb. He'd been pastor of the nondenominational New Canaan Bible Church for some thirty years before stepping down ... telling his congregation he needed "time to resolve some things that are going on in my personal life."

There was more.

> Two years ago, Newcomb led members of his congregation to Montpelier to protest the state's Civil Union law ... "We're going to storm the capitol," Newcomb told a reporter. "I'm praying there will be bus loads and bus loads of people to show their opposition to this madness."

So much for compartmentalizing. Everything I had so neatly packed away came spewing out. I felt sick remembering how Reggie bared his teeth pretending to smile, how I stood dumbstruck when he informed me the Lord led him into my house. I felt sickest remembering four-year-old Noah wandering freely, exploring the woods behind our house, making forts under the drooping hydrangea branches. While Noah had been a brave explorer, Reggie had been living right next door, molesting children.

But remember, allegations are just that. Not facts. (Yet). I tried to quiet my runaway fear; *innocent until proven guilty . . .* and all that. I'd tried to make a joke of it so I wouldn't be scared, but it just wasn't funny, not any more. If it ever had been. Because now he was accused of molesting children. *Little boys?*

So I did what I'd done the first time, I called the police. I realized that my suspicions that Reggie had stolen my jewelry might not have any bearing on the current charges, but I didn't care. I already had the phone in my hand, determined to tell my story. I didn't want to have it clanging around in my head, and I didn't want to ignore it, and I was sick of trying to turn it into a joke.

The policeman in charge of the case was courteous and vaguely interested, a little more sophisticated than the last one, so he didn't burst out enthusiastically—as if he'd learned to talk like a policeman from watching cop shows on TV. No "We've got our man!" from him. Instead he explained, "I've talked to Reverend Newcomb a great deal over the course of the investigation and I get the feeling he is in the mood to come clean about a lot of things in his life." He agreed that this might indeed be a good time to ask again about the missing jewelry, and promised he'd do it. I was breathing a silent thank you when, almost as an afterthought, the policeman asked if I wanted to contact Reggie myself.

"Can I do that?"

"Yes, of course, you certainly can."

I considered this all the next day, embarrassed that I'd needed someone in authority to make the suggestion, to give me permission. I'd been so concerned about being neighborly and trying not to make Reggie mad, that *I'd* shut myself up. Enough of this talking to the police. I had some things I wanted to say right to Reggie.

I'd write a letter. But how do you talk to someone who you know is a thief—even if it's never been proven—and who's an alleged child molester? I knew exactly what I wanted to say, even though I'd never say most of it. But I still had to seize this moment and try to get my jewelry back.

I had to get the tone right, sincere and non-threatening, on the slim chance that Reggie would understand what the loss had meant to me. If he had a modicum of decency, if he was trying to make things right with his God, maybe, just maybe, I'd see my mother's jewelry again.

> *Dear Reggie,*
>
> *I'm writing to ask you to help me locate the jewelry that was taken from my home during the time I was your neighbor. You remember that I sold you my car and that you went in my house when I wasn't there to get the title. Given this situation I'm sure you can understand why I might think you or someone in your family might have seen the jewelry and taken it. This jewelry is of great sentimental value to me. It was given to me by my mother before she died. I ask you to search your conscience and perhaps ask your family if any one of them ever took anything from my home. If the jewelry is found and returned to me, I can assure you that will be the end of the matter; no questions asked. I don't wish to make your life any more difficult than it must be at this time. I'd appreciate your help in resolving this theft.*

I didn't expect to hear anything for a while, or maybe ever. But in just a couple of days I got a letter back.

> *Dear Jesse,*
>
> *I talked to my son once again about your missing jewelry and again he stated that he had never gone into your home for anything. I believe the theft to have occurred by your former roommate. I believe the two of you had just parted company and she would be the most likely suspect to want to hurt you. Why would my son or I want to do you any harm? As God is my witness and judge we had absolutely nothing to do with this theft. I'm deeply grieved that you have suspected us all these years.*

"Why would my son or I want to do you any harm? . . . I am deeply grieved . . ." Now I wasn't angry anymore. No, now I was furious. It wasn't just the jewelry; this was no longer about things. This had evolved into something far more personal. I'd seen this before: bigots ignore the reality that what they believe, what they say, hurts people. As if these are just ideas in a vacuum that don't cause pain, that don't damage real people.

I had more to say.

> Reggie,
>
> I must correct some mistakes you made in your letter. First, the woman you so carefully call my roommate, was my lover. We did not part company until one year after the theft so accusing her as you did makes no sense. Second, you wonder why I would think that you would want to harm me. Let me tell you. When I first moved to New Canaan, I was well aware of your attitudes towards gay people. What do you think I would feel when you are quoted in the press saying things like, "I'm praying there will be bus loads and bus loads of people to show their opposition to this madness" about the Civil Union law? In spite of what you think and preach you do not own God. Any loving union between gay people is as blessed by God as is your heterosexual marriage. Now, at long last, our unions also have the blessing of the State of Vermont. Is it clear to you now why I have believed all these years that you did not wish me well?

Forget being neighborly and polite. Forget the benefit-of-the-doubt, innocent-until-proven-guilty. It's obvious I'm never going to see that jewelry again. But finally I'd stood up to Reggie and I wasn't afraid any more. I'd told the truth, and that was enough.

Every once in a while I wonder what it would be like to live with beliefs as absolute and unassailable as Reggie's. Maybe that makes it easier to live in a world where people aren't who they appear to be, where things happen that don't make any sense. Maybe I could even get myself to believe that the Lord has a personal hand in everything, so you don't have to be responsible for what you do. Maybe I could even convince myself that the Lord led me to Reggie to learn these important lessons.

Maybe.

Or maybe it suits me better to live with the messiness, and mystery and monsters that can slither out of our own murky swamps. That's what unassailable truth protects you from, isn't it, the swamp monsters?

I do know for sure that saying those things to Reggie, even so long after the fact, helped. My anger at him had almost burned itself out.

What was left, like ashes and rubble after a house burns down, was being mad at my mother. Like the way a kid gets mad: *How could you do this to me? How could you leave me alone in this messy world, peopled with Reggies? I need you to help me sort this out.*

Now that I understand this I feel lighter, ready to go back to living without my mother's jewelry. The gold ring and the bright blue brooch, they're just *things*, after all. I'm ready to go on, remembering my mother, and how much fun we had telling each other stories over the phone.

Now that I'm not as mad it's a lot easier to remember.

Dropped Stitch

4

Dropped Stitch

I've been surrounded by knitters my entire life. My mother spent a lifetime trying to teach me—"Jesse, it's so relaxing, you'll be able to make tiny sweaters for my grandbabies" (*who I'll never get to see*, is what she didn't say out loud)—making her final attempt from her deathbed. Later I surrounded myself with a group of women who knit, though I didn't know it at the time.

Counting me, there are five of us who've been getting together once a month to share a meal and talk. Once a month for the past fifteen years. That's one hundred and eighty get-togethers. At three hours per session that's a lot of talking. And listening. These four friends have knitted their way through all of these stories that I'm about to tell you.

How we became a group is as good a way as any to begin.

As you know, I was living in New Canaan village, a lovely place for heterosexual couples fleeing cities, seeking a certain quality of life for their children. But this turned out not to be such a happy place for a newly single parent, a *lesbian* mother, at that. The lesbian part put me even farther out at the edge, even more than being a "flatlander" did. My life was full with work and four-and-a-half year old Noah and I was just pregnant with the as-yet-unnamed Sophie. (*And where is the invisible father—who is he?*—I'm sure these questions provided some juicy gossip at the general store.)

But something was missing. Where were the best friends?

One morning making Noah's breakfast, slapping batter in the pan, ferociously flipping pancakes, I realized I was mad, really mad. Noah hadn't done anything wrong, I was looking forward to the new baby's coming, but something wasn't right. What was it?

Dammit, I'm lonely.

So, I was single, I'd accepted that. My mother wasn't alive to help me bring my baby home, I was living with that. But where were women friends that I could gather around me like a billowing skirt? I just knew there was a group of marvelous women who got together to share their most intimate thoughts and that, somehow, they'd forgotten to invite me to join them.

Jeez, why didn't they call me?

Okay, fine. I'll start a group myself.

And so I did.

In the beginning we were a baker's dozen, thirteen. We didn't have a topic or a structure or even a name. Just ourselves. And, in spite of our combined brainpower, the name we chose for ourselves was The Women's Group. Over the years we grew smaller, so now these fifteen years later, we are just five. But we're still The Women's Group.

Let me introduce you:

Carla, is the oldest of us at sixty-four. She raised six kids alone after her husband committed suicide. She's our resident expert on all child-rearing questions, developmental issues, sibling rivalry, when to put your foot down and say "enough's enough." And on surviving grief. Carla is a midwife and when we met at my first prenatal appointment, I knew I'd met someone who was a truth teller—and someone who would help me tell the truth—because after she'd finished the exam she asked me, "So what's the story with this baby's father?" and I told her.

Maggie's a midwife too. I called her when I went into labor with Sophie and she ran into the delivery suite at three in the morning, wearing the most beautiful Guatemalan dress. She arrived just in time to catch Sophie, who "flew out after two pushes, like squeezed toothpaste," Maggie said, as she wrapped my new baby in a soft cotton blanket and placed her on my chest.

Julia's a psychologist who works with special needs children and their families. We met right after my mother died, and she listened to my outpouring of grief, like she had all the time in the world. She has an extraordinary ability to say the most profound things in the simplest way.

Lizanne is a sign language interpreter. She often signs when she's talking in our group, without intending to, because she's so fluently bilingual. Her signing somehow expands and deepens what she's saying, even though none of us understands American Sign Language.

And then there's me.

We have seen so many changes over all these years—divorces, marriages, deaths—but one thing has remained a constant. All of them knit. They bring their yarn, needles, and patterns to every meeting. As soon as the eating is over, the patterns come out and the knitting begins. I watch the creation of beautiful, intricate sweaters while we talk. I'm the only one who doesn't knit. I envy their creativity, their skill, but—I'm embarrassed to admit—sometimes I'm jealous of the attention the knitting gets when it's my turn to talk. I want their undivided attention. I try to focus on their expertise, remembering how much my mother loved the soothing rhythm of the needles. But, at the same time, I do wish they'd finish making sweaters for other people, and knit one for me.

Last month, during our meeting one of the knitters ran into a technical problem and, right in the middle of whatever she was telling us, she interrupted herself to ask the others for help. I didn't understand the problem, but I could see the solution, because it was enacted right there in front of me. She began to unravel an almost-finished deep teal sleeve.

I didn't mean to, but I couldn't stop myself, "Why are you doing that?" The unraveler glanced up at me, reacting to my alarm more than to the task at hand. "It's okay," she said, "it's just a dropped stitch."

Just? Like it's that easy to re-do, make it right?
My dropped stitches haven't been that easy.

Take Brenda; she didn't seem like she'd ever become anything other than the sparkling, gregarious, six foot tall woman I was charmed by when we met. She'd just moved to Vermont with her seven-year-old son, Thomas, having fled a disastrous marriage, confident she'd arrived at the beginning of a new life. (I guess lots of us flatlanders arrive in the north country nurturing that fantasy.) Anyway, chemistry drew us together, overriding all sense or caution. Noah was in kindergarden, Sophie was just an infant, and I was sick of being a single parent. At the instant Brenda took the baby into her arms declaring "I'm Sophie's other mama" I knew my world had changed forever.

In the beginning everything was enchanted. I was blinded by the pleasure of my new family, so I didn't recognize that Thomas had adopted the role of problem child. No doubt once he'd been a real bones and blood boy, but by the time we met, he was a vortex sucking up everything in his path. Defiance and rage were his game; I became his target and rival.

Simple things became complicated at his hand: "Thomas, please stop fiddling with the stove door, you could break it." The stove was the first thing we had to get fixed.

He was smart about people, though, and got my number immediately. Zeroing in on me, he dangled a hook baited with hate, and I—I'm ashamed to admit—I bit. Not a flattering picture, a grown woman locked in deadly rivalry with a seven-year-old boy in desperate pursuit of a coveted prize. Brenda.

And Thomas zeroed in on Noah too, informing him of a new reality: "You're a wimp. You dork, you can't even throw a baseball." Which was true but had never been a problem before. Snarling, "Nobody reads all the time like that."

But he played with Sophie, picking her up and swinging her in circles while she shrieked, fear mixed with delight. By the time she was five she'd lived with Thomas all her remembered life, idolizing him as the perfect big brother.

Later, our relationship in tatters, after everything that happened, Brenda moved out with Thomas, leaving me alone in a house so big that the three of us rattled in the emptiness. Leaving me to pick up the pieces of the family we'd pretended to be.

So many dropped stitches. I've been so busy taking care of every day business, just getting through the day, that I never realized what happens if you ignore them. Hoping they'd disappear. But now, these many years later, well, they're still there.

Unchanged.

First I have to find them all. Then I can start the work of unraveling. Then knitting them back in. I'm hoping the pieces will fit together seamlessly. Maybe they will.

But probably the whole will never be flawless. Because of all that's gone on before, it will probably be riddled with imperfections. One thing's for sure: when I'm done knitting this time—alpaca, wool, or cotton—the whole may not be perfect. It will be something better. It will be true.

Family Business

5

The Family Business

MY MOTHER'S PEOPLE WERE in business. Her father, Shmuel (later he would become Sam), was a poor Jewish boy who grew up on the Lower East Side. He didn't have money, but what he did have was plenty of *chutzpah*. A typical story. Sam married young and after trying his hand in his father-in-law's grocery store, he set his sights higher and borrowed $500—which felt like a fortune to him—to start a paint business. Borrowing to finance a dream: it was a common enough story for those times. What was uncommon was what came next: the company he started prospered so he and his new wife, Crystal (she started life as Goldie), emerged from the Depression having made, not lost, a small fortune. They left their class behind without even a single glance back, having achieved a small piece of the American dream. "Nouveau riche." If you said it right, even the term jingled like money. Grandpa Sam cast his eye about for a new challenge and found it in politics. He ran for office on the Democratic ticket, more out of pragmatism than any deep conviction, and before he'd even imagined it possible, he was mayor of their small town, which was near enough to New York City to have a noticeable Jewish minority, but provincial enough to still be solidly anti-Semitic.

As mayor he finally had the status he craved. He took his stylish wife and five small children to synagogue on the High Holidays, more to show off their holiday finery and to *kibbitz* with his political cronies than out of any religious conviction. His father had been an Orthodox Jew from the old country, but Sam didn't want to have anything to do with that old world stuff, he just wanted to fit in.

He loved a challenge. Learning the ropes, exercising influence, that was what demanded his attention. But Sam was new to power. Who knows what he did to cause his relations with the local police union to sour?

Maybe nothing. Maybe he was just a Jew.

Early one sunny Monday morning after his five children had left for school, after he'd had his breakfast coffee and bagel with lox and cream cheese in the elegant dining room with his still slim and stylish wife, he was shot to death by a disgruntled policeman. Witnesses heard the shots and they heard White—that was the murderous officer's name—screaming, "Jew-bastard!" They saw him kicking my grandfather long after the gun hung empty in his hand. They saw Grandma Crystal cradling his bloody head in her lap, wailing in uncomprehending grief. A crowd gathered around what was now a corpse, watching helplessly, as Grandpa Sam's blood seeped into the pavement.

Sam died young, leaving behind an even younger wife and the children he had never taken the time to know, too busy making business deals, finagling, exercising power. But he wasn't too busy to try to create an heir, and after two previous attempts (failures) to produce a son, my mother, Gloria, came along, having committed the original sin of not being a boy. He never let her forget it. She tried. She changed her name to Bobbie, but it wasn't enough. She was fifteen when her father bled to death on the sidewalk of the street that would be named for him as a permanent memorial.

Sam had earned a reputation as a bit of a conniver who hoarded his money, hoping to avoid taxes or provide for his family, it wasn't clear which. Anyway, he had the foresight to consult lawyers to plan for the future he'd never see, placing the business in trust for us, the as-yet-unborn grandchildren. That's what we heard when we were growing up, "The business belongs to the grandchildren." We didn't know what it meant exactly, but it sounded mysterious, tantalizing. The sound of money. Someday we'd be business owners, too.

My father's people were intellectuals and writers; teaching and writing was their family business. Grandfather Solomon was a minor author, who earned a meager living by working for the Jewish Welfare Board. I don't know that Grandmother Esther made a living at it, but she wrote at an astonishing rate, churning out at least two books a year. Both were "Jewish writers," focusing on Jewish history, philosophy, and biographies of famous Jews.

Like Grandpa Sam, Grandfather Solomon grew up poor. But he didn't dream of money, his energies were devoted to getting an education. Solomon earned a full scholarship and a PhD in philosophy, unusual for anyone, but especially a poor Jew, in the early part of the century. Craving the status attached to the title "professor," he longed to teach, but since university jobs were scarce (how much did quotas limit his options?) he'd had to settle for becoming a rabbi. When he finally finished his studies and had to face the reality that he couldn't find work, he volunteered for the Army, serving in France during the First World War, a chaplain to boys in the trenches. Grandpa Solomon wrote a book about his war experiences, never mentioning that while he was ministering to injured or dying Jewish boys, his wife was home, grieving the death of one of their infant twins, the baby Moses. The flu epidemic of 1918 took Moses and though my grandmother survived, she was never *right* afterwards. The living twin, Judith, was bereft her entire life.

Grandmother Esther's books were not scholarly philosophy or theory. Instead, she aimed at making Jewish education entertaining and engaging, a novel approach in those days. She didn't "have a job"—she stayed at home with her children, of course—but found time to write more than thirty books; biographies, plays and children's stories. We had two entire shelves of books by Silvermans in the bookcases that lined our family room.

My mother tolerated Grandfather Solomon—she didn't much like him—though somehow she took good care of him during his last years when he came to live with us. But she hated my grandmother. I don't know how I knew this exactly. She certainly never said so directly. But I inhaled it the few times she mentioned Esther by name. Usually she said "your grandmother" or even more damning, "your father's mother."

In part, she blamed Esther for what she felt was wrong with my father—that he wasn't very communicative or warm. (She must have felt like she was in a desert, engulfed in all that silence.) Later on, after all us kids had left home and she was alone with my father, she really got fed up with his silences. "Speak to me, oh sage," she'd demand, equal parts admiration and goading. He'd look stumped (*what have I done wrong*? his expression said) and then come up with some comment, hoping it would satisfy. She described all the Silvermans—my father, his sister and their parents, as "too goddamn intellectual."

Later she told me stories that helped fill in some of the blanks, though really all the episodes were variations on the same theme —the care-about-all-the-wrong-things-too-goddamn-intellectual theme. This particular story sums it up: Grandmother Esther was visiting us at our house outside New Orleans, Louisiana, where we moved when my father got his first university job. My mother had her hands full. She was pregnant with me, constantly nauseous from the misnamed *morning* sickness, spending most of her time hoping not to throw up, struggling to keep up with my brother, Benny, her first-born, a wiry, energetic four-year-old.

Names had weight in our family. Benny was named for my father's brother, Benjamin, Esther's oldest son. A mythological figure, he had volunteered to fight with the Abraham Lincoln Brigade during the Spanish Civil War, and was killed in Spain, just twenty years old. He was a writer, too, sending home stories and poems so vivid they made his comrades, the Spanish resistance, and even the countryside come alive. Benjamin was a powerful presence—the family hero, what we should all aspire to—but my father never really said much about him. Except that he ran away when he was fourteen, and when he was dragged back home he became the fastest long-distance runner his high school had ever seen. My father was fifteen when his brother died fighting the good fight.

That history hovered over little Benny's head. When my father arrived home from the train station with my grandmother, my mother woke Benny from his nap. "They're here, it's time to say hello to your Grandma." Jerking awake, Benny ran, skipping, leaping, flying down the driveway to welcome her. Benny was a fast runner, too, and Brownie, the family dog, trotted along, trying to keep up, caught up in the excitement. My mother trailed behind, watching proudly. Grandmother Esther bent down, her arms stretched open, cooing, "Oh, oh, isn't he cute."

With that, she threw her arms around the little brown dog, greeting him with kisses.

My mother never got over it.

I started to write when I was seven, poetry mostly. But it was a secret private pleasure. I wrote bits and scribbles—often started, seldom finished—on the backs of envelopes and in journal after journal, for the next thirty years. I didn't show my scribbling to anyone. Worry panted hot down my neck when I wrote—*what's safe to say, what's off limits? How do I fictionalize enough to tell all these stories that were begging to be told?*

What I did know with utmost clarity was that writing was a risky proposition. Danger lurked, I might violate unwritten rules, I couldn't afford to take any chances.

I loved my mother desperately. How could I betray her by becoming anything like my grandmother? How could I be a writer?

I can see now, looking back, that I studied psychology, becoming a psychotherapist who practiced "the talking cure," to try to help other people tell *their* stories. And I was pretty good at it. Hundreds of stories later, after uncountable hours of listening, new realities forced me into early retirement. Untethered from my career and my identity as a listener, I floundered, unable to imagine anything that would ever be as engaging, challenging, right for me.

Maybe my appointment with Vincent, the psychic I consulted when I turned forty (I'll fill you in soon on what he said about my past lives and how he predicted my future) maybe that consultation cracked me open, paving the way for Dorothy, the last in a long string of therapists I'd seen. Dorothy didn't talk like a therapist, she sounded more like a shaman, and, even stranger to my ears, she used astrology to illustrate her points. *Astrology? What am I doing talking with this woman?*

Dorothy was "centered," and assured me that when I finished therapy with her I'd arrive at my own centering, having discovered what my new *right work* was. Silently, I scoffed. Despairing. Impossible to imagine I'd ever find other work that I would care about as much. Or be as good at.

Dorothy talked like a psychic but acted like an English professor: she required all her clients to write. Writing was not optional. So for two years I wrote every day, filling page after page, notebook after notebook. When I was done with therapy-writing, I couldn't stop. I started to create short stories—very short—and when I was finished with those, I discovered I needed to write longer ones. Not convinced I had anything much to say, those longer stories were still short, strangely truncated. But the actual fact of composing them was satisfying beyond my wildest fantasies.

Dorothy was "on-the-money," as my mother would've said. Because by the time my work with her was done, I understood that my future was about going back to pick up those dropped stitches. *Right work* or not, this had become a necessity, driven by an almost physical urgency.

But what about that unnamed threat: tsunami or volcano? Water or fire? Inside or outside? The risks, the consequences, of stepping over some invisible boundary and landing in one of the swamps I had spent my life tiptoeing around, that still loomed. But I really didn't have a choice anymore. I had to do it. It was in my blood. Because now, I could not *not* write.

6

Naming Ourselves

I NEVER LIKED MY LAST name. It just never felt like it fit me. But I didn't do anything about it, because it never occurred to me that it was possible to change something so basic. As I've told you before, names had weight in our family. I was afraid if I changed the name inherited from my father, that would be interpreted as dishonoring him, and not only him, but the entire Silverman family. Even though most of them were dead, that didn't mean they couldn't exert psychic power over me. So I never considered taking matters into my own hands and molding my name to fit me better. I figured that you were stuck for life with what you'd been given.

My mother's name was Gloria, but everyone called her Glo, except my father who called her Glochick. It wasn't like him to use that kind of sexist language and I silently held it against him until, years later, I realized that it was *chik,* the Yiddish term of affection. Our Jewishness made its appearance in our lives in such indirect ways, so subtle I often didn't recognize it for what it was. A term of endearment here, a *poch en tuchas* there.

My mother never liked her name either. So she named me Jesse (spelled the boy-way), "because it didn't sound one iota like Gloria," which was the name in fashion when *her* mother was naming *her.* She told me there were three other Glorias in her first-grade class alone. To distinguish herself from the crowd she called herself Bobbie. Whether this was a rejection of her name or gender, or both, I don't know. When I asked about this one day she said, "Well, my father wanted a boy and I tried hard to please him. It never worked. But anyway, boys just seemed to have more fun."

I have to agree with her about that.

When she died I inherited her tiny gold pinkie ring with her initials engraved on it. GBE. The B in the center is the biggest. Except there's no B in her real name. That B is for Bobbie.

My mother settled on Jesse for me, which I kind of liked, except since she'd used the spelling for a boy's name the teachers always looked up, surprised when a short, little girl with out-of-control black hair shouted out "Here!" during roll call. That was me, trying to live up to my outlaw name.

So when Noah was four, and my second child was still unborn, I began playing with female names. I just *knew* the baby would be a girl. By the time she was born—even though she made her appearance a full three weeks early—I was ready, with her name all picked out. I would never burden her with a male-sounding name, even if mine had given me the courage to adopt a wild, outsider stance. I'd learned by then that Ashkenazi Jews don't name children after living relatives. I considered giving her a B name for brave Bobbie, but even with the 'ie' it sounded too boyish. I narrowed the search down to names that had a kind of Old Testament resonance to connect her to her roots. I wanted Sarah, after my favorite aunt who'd just come out to the entire family by appearing at the very front of a Gay Pride march on national TV, carrying one side of a rainbow banner proclaiming GAY AND PROUD PROFESSORS FOR PEACE. I liked that name's biblical roots, and now its most recent political connection. But my brother Jon—who by now had changed his name to Jonnie and would later become Jack—had already chosen Sarah for his daughter. I tried to deal graciously with the recognition that he had beaten me again, as he had at everything when we were growing up. He'd gotten to Sarah first.

I chose Sophie.

There was still a middle name. Maybe I could find one to carry just the right amount of weight. Mine is Edwards, my mother's maiden name. But more trouble lurked here. This name was undoubtedly changed at Ellis Island, Edjuvisky, I think it was. But by the time it got to me it was used to tease and torture. "Jesse, Jesse, Eddie, Eddie! What kind of name is that for a girl?"

No male-sounding middle names for my baby daughter. No "maiden" names either.

And then it came to me. Glory. Glory for her Grandma. Glory for me. Glory to celebrate her.

Sophie Glory Silverman. Born June 12, 1990. It wasn't from the Bible exactly, but it had a biblical feel.

A name you could live with.

The year Sophie turned five our lives blew apart, hers most of all. I've mentioned that the bottom fell out of her world precipitously when Brenda, the only other mother she'd ever known, moved out, taking Thomas with her. Sophie demanded the truth. "Why doesn't Be-Be" (her baby name for Brenda) "love me anymore?" All my patient explaining, "You didn't do anything wrong, this is a grown-up problem between Brenda and me" didn't do a damn thing to comfort her. She didn't believe a word of it, sinking into a child's version of hell, her only consolation being to start sucking her thumb again.

I took her to a child therapist where she spent an expensive hour once a week sitting on a tastefully carpeted floor scribbling with a black magic marker. After a couple of months of shrieking protest, "I hate going there. I hate it so much!" I realized I couldn't force her to confront her wounds. She would decide when—if ever—to face her demons.

Slowly over the next couple of years the old Sophie re-emerged, and by the time she was seven, she was the kid I remembered, the pre-five Sophie, the kid who looked up at me one morning when I was helping her put on her coat, and said, with a straight face, "You are an evil midget!" dissolving in raucous laughter at her own great joke.

But we were still patching our lives back together when I fell in love with Anna, and when she started to spend the night, Sophie was none too happy.

First she attacked Anna's looks: "Who is she? She looks like a hitchhiker."

Later, "Why does she have to stay over?" and, "What do you mean, she raises goats? Oh, yeah, so that's why she acts like a farmer!" which simply translated meant, *If I have to share you, why doesn't Brenda come back, so my life can go on being the way it was before?*

Disgust gave way to ignoring, which segued into curiosity—*maybe those goats are pretty cool, after all, especially the babies*— "they're called kids, just like me," which, after a couple of years, morphed into something entirely different. Maybe love.

Then one early morning just before her ninth birthday Sophie announced, "I'm going to change my name."

Oh?

"From now on I'm going to be Sophie Glory Rosewood Silverman, because Anna is my other Mommy, and I'm part of her family."

Really? "Okay."

So I called around to find out how to change a name. We filled out paperwork, and went for an appointment with the judge in her chambers, Sophie, Anna, and I. Judge Gates asked each of us a few questions; then she smiled and signed the form to change Sophie's name. The new name wouldn't be legal until it'd been published in the newspaper for a week, then it would be official.

We went out for ice cream to celebrate, even though it was the middle of December.

Sophie wanted to give Anna a Mommy-gift. She picked out a stone with a carved heart that she'd painted red. She just knew for sure Anna would carry it in her pocket always. Anna gave Sophie a silver bracelet with gold Kokopeli dancers engraved on it. I took pictures of them posing with their gifts, hugging each other. Then we took Sophie back to school, where she told her third-grade class that Anna had adopted her, and now she had two mommies.

Sophie Glory Rosewood Silverman.

Oh, well. There goes the biblical resonance.

It took me a while, but I figured it out. I had a good teacher. If Sophie could take matters into her own hands without worrying about her parents, I could too.

A couple of months after Sophie changed her name, my new name found me. It leapt off the page of a book—I was already Jesse (*thanks, Bobbie*). Now I would add Silver, a lean version of the name inherited from my father. When I'm writing, doing my new right work, I wrap my chosen name around me like a prayer shawl, a *tallit*. Jesse Silver. Perfect fit.

7

Learning to Swim

My brother Jon never learned to swim as well as the rest of us, but I'm not sure exactly why. Maybe it was because when our mother taught me to swim in the pool with the murky water at our cheap hotel outside of Cuernavaca, Mexico, when I was five, Jon was only three-and-a-half, and she never got around to him. Or maybe it was because I took to water so naturally that she thought she didn't really have to teach her children, we'd just pick it up by ourselves. Or maybe it's that Jon's the one most like our father, two brilliant scientists, both living esoteric, intellectual lives, absent from their bodies. Watching them swim is almost painful; it's never certain that they'll arrive where they've set out for.

In contrast, I'm a wonderful swimmer, even more at home in the water than on land. Which has been a source of pleasure and pride my whole life. I thank my mother for it, although, just like she thought, I'm sure I would have learned on my own, it came so naturally.

Once, when Brenda and I were still together, I invited Jon and his wife and young daughter to join us for a week-long family vacation. Actually this was not my idea at all, since I'd felt quite distant from him for many years. Not that there'd been a major falling out—that I'd understood anyway—just that we'd drifted apart when we were teenagers and I'd had a hard time re-connecting with the man he'd become. He had a habit of lecturing about his microbiology research in a loud voice, talking in exquisite detail about science that I had no hope of understanding. I'd listen, trying to act interested, and then ease my way out of the room. He never did seem to notice that his audience had left.

Brenda had met Jon at a family get-together, and liked him. They had a lot in common: a love of cooking and of talking. They were both big people, with big voices and big opinions. They shouted at each other, enthusiastically, without any apparent need for the other to listen.

They were both a mystery to me.

Anyway, she wanted Jon to come. We'd rented a big old beach house on Lake George with plenty of bedrooms. We could cook, and eat, and go canoeing, and swim.

I was at that place in our relationship where I was still trying to please Brenda, even though I knew that things had gone bad. But I couldn't acknowledge how bad it was, and in my desperate attempt to keep her, I was doing anything she wanted. So I invited Jon.

We all arrived at the same time from our various states, and almost immediately Jon and Brenda moved into the kitchen. The rest of us, relieved of kitchen duties, gathered the kids and ran down the long lawn to the sandy beach. The kids played in the shallow water, picking up snail shells. We grown-ups settled into lawn chairs, while the kids splashed and built sand castles and got sunburned. Then we all went back up to the house, set the oval dining room table, and ate the wonderful meal that somehow Brenda and Jon had produced.

We all ate, and drank and had coffee after dinner, and then after-dinner drinks. Then the rest of us teamed up for clean up, before going back to the beach to watch the sunset.

We'd established a comfortable rhythm for a lazy vacation week. We all ate too much, but that seemed like a good idea since it was vacation. Whenever we needed a break from too much food, or kids, someone would go off to take a nap. Nothing exciting, just family time.

The day before we were going to leave, Jon asked me if I'd like to go for a swim with him. I seriously considered saying no, because it seemed like it wouldn't be a lot of fun to have to watch him the whole time, just to make sure he didn't go under. Plus, I'd have to ask Brenda to watch Sophie and Noah, which didn't seem like it'd be a lot of fun either. But I couldn't remember the last time Jon asked me to do anything with him, so I did it.

I told him I'd go, but I couldn't stop myself from saying, "Do you feel safe? I know swimming's not really your thing. Can you tell me if you get tired and we'll head for shore?"

"Sure," he nodded as we waded into the warm lake.

"Where do you want to go?" I asked him as we started off with an easy breaststroke, me watching him out of the corner of my eye. He seemed okay so far.

"There," he said, pointing to an island straight ahead of us, but at least a mile away. "Let's swim to the island. We can take a rest if we need to and then swim back."

Okay, I'm game. He's my little brother, but he's a grown man now, and he must know what he's doing. So we swam along together, matching each other stroke for stroke, in companionable silence.

Midway, Jon began to talk: "Why, do you think, we had such different experiences growing up with Mom? Because, you know, we're so close in age, but we think of her in such different ways." I was still grieving for our mother who had died five years before.

And so, out there in the water, without land to stand on, we talked about growing up together, about how, now in middle age with our own children, we saw our mother so differently. We got to the island, where we shared secrets.

And when Jon caught his breath, we swam back. We arrived on the little beach, seeing each other a little differently.

I understood more about the teenager he'd been, who I'd never been able to figure out. And I could see the man he'd become, who, somehow, when I wasn't paying attention, had learned to swim.

The Little Girl

8

Bezel

n. the faceted part of a cut gem that rises above the setting

I'VE ALREADY TOLD YOU how I'd begun therapy with yet-again-another-therapist, Dorothy, who came with superlative recommendations. Except no one told me she talked like a shaman. Plus, she didn't call what she did *therapy*. No, it was The Healing Path. And she, herself, wasn't a counselor or therapist, she was my Guide. Dorothy's primary modality was astrology, something I'd given barely a passing thought to except for maybe an occasional scan of my horoscope in the daily paper, followed by a scoff. But here I was lying on a couch, a pillow under my legs to help me relax. *Relax? Who can relax when someone's talking to you in language you barely understand? I mean, it's English, but I only make sense of about half of what she says. Now she's murmuring about "The Sacred Wound." Wounded, I understand, but what could possibly make it sacred?*

I know. I've got it: it's the result of a ritual stabbing practiced by some ancient, indigenous peoples in a godforsaken desert or dripping rain forest. But when I start to ask about the sacred wound— *what are we talking about here exactly?*—she uses astrology to illustrate her point, explaining patiently that my south node is conjunct my Mars and Neptune, that I silence myself in order to protect myself from Pluto in my 12th house. I've always resisted theory as too constricting, but this doesn't sound even vaguely like theory. It sounds like gobbledygook. I listen to be polite, but her words wash over, leaving me dazed and numb. This doesn't help me understand myself at all. It just makes me sleepy.

Dorothy's still going on about my sacred wound; I'm drifting. When I force myself to tune back in, I have a new problem. Because even when I manage to push the indigenous people dancing around the fire off to the side, my inner critic starts chattering away: *Sacred wound? South node? Are you kidding me? What is this woman talking about?* The noise in my head is so loud I can hardly make out what she's saying.

Not only do we discuss wounds and nodes—well, Dorothy does, I complain silently to myself—we do breath work. This, at least, I find I can manage. My many years doing yoga help here. I can let myself breathe deeply, lying flat with a pillow under my knees while Dorothy sits beside me, guiding the rhythm.

Inhale, exhale. Slowly. Inhale, exhale, again.

And that's when I see her.

There she is, five years old, entirely herself, standing on the platform at the railway station. I inch forward slowly, quietly, so I don't frighten her. I lean over, bending close, to hear what she's trying to say. I try to memorize every word, just as she tells it to me.

We are at home, having supper, when some big boys come and bang loudly on the door. When Mama doesn't get there right away, they burst in shouting. We hide behind her, my little sister and I, but we hear exactly what they are screaming: "Jew, out!" They run through our apartment, throwing everything on the floor and knocking our family pictures off the mantel. There's the crash of glass breaking and

they laugh and yell as they step on the shattered photographs and dishes and kick everything around with their big boots. Mama tries to hide us but they just push past her, knocking her down as they run out the door, screaming. "Jewdogs, scum!"

Mama looks stern, she tells us to pack a suitcase. I want to take my little stuffed animal, she's a kitty and she's never been away from me before. Mama says it's okay, but to hurry, hurry.

She throws some clothes into a suitcase for my sister. I'm five-and-three-quarters and big enough to pack for myself. I take some things—don't know what. And I hug Sadie, my kitten, inside my coat, holding her tight because she's scared.

We practically fall down the stairs we're rushing so fast, and out into the cold. It's dark, there are people everywhere on the street. We're shoved along with them, everyone crowded together in a crush, moving toward the station. Mama is holding my hand tight, dragging me along and she's carrying Hannah, my baby sister. Papa isn't with us; he's been away all week.

When we get to the station, Mama suddenly lets go my hand, there are so many people pushing and going in all directions, shouting. I am smushed up against people I don't know. All I can see is coats and legs. I can hardly breathe we're pressed so tight together. I try to call out, "Mama, Mama!" but I can barely make a sound. I can't catch my breath. I don't have my suitcase anymore; all I have is Sadie snuggling close inside my coat. My nose is dripping; I wipe it on my sleeve, even though Mama says it's rude not to use a handkerchief.

How can my Mama leave me like this? Did I do something bad? Why did those boys come screaming into our house? And why did Mama let go of me? Did I make her mad and that's why? How will I find Mama and baby Hannah? What will happen to me and Sadie alone like this with all these strangers crushed together on the platform? Where's my Mama? Who will look after me and Sadie now?

She stares at me, wide-eyed, exhausted, out of breath.

"Who are you?"

"My name is Petra."

I stare back at her, not recognizing the name, I've never heard it before. But I recognize the expression, I've seen it on my own face. How did it happen that here, breathing deeply, I've met a little girl who just might be the most important person in my life? Who is she? Past life bleed-through? That's what Dorothy might say. The result of an over-active imagination? Reading too much Holocaust literature, maybe? Some shred of my own lost self?

I have no idea. But what's beyond doubt is that she's there, waiting for me. How have I been able to shut her away for a lifetime?

And what do I do now to reassure her, to promise that she is welcome here? Home with me at last. What words can possibly convey that final, that ultimate, sacred vow? That I will never, ever let go her hand.

9

Ice

IN YET ANOTHER IN a series of breathwork sessions with Dorothy—*inhale, exhale*—*Damn, what's that?* I stumbled over something icy inside. I'd already met the little girl, Petra, and welcomed her home. That encounter, added to years of therapy before I ever met her, had me convinced that I knew all there was to know about my interior life. *What am I going to discover next?* I thought this was my final go-around, just checking to make sure everything was fine, polish off any rough spots.

Eyes squeezed tight, I squinted into the deep freeze. I could just make out a small child, crouching, hugging herself, braced against the cold. *Was that her again, that persistent little girl?* Just seeing her shivering, I was tugged by that old familiar undertow. *All I want to do was go to bed and cry. I just wish she felt acknowledged enough to stay away. Please can't you leave me alone?* Then I remembered my promise not to ignore her, that she needed me to warm her. *Okay, I'll take care of you because I promised (but will you ever be satisfied?).*

She needed me, but so did Noah and Sophie, my real children, with their own needs and demands, so I couldn't go to bed. Distracted, focused inside, I went through the motions of ordinary life, pretending everything was fine.

This involved getting Noah out of bed and suggesting—trying to use my most reasonable tone of voice—that he start studying for his final exams. Sophie's best friend Jennifer had slept over. When they got up, bleary-eyed, they wanted pancakes and to bounce on the trampoline and to watch TV and to go bowling and....

I made the pancakes, they watched TV. Who knows what Noah was doing? *Should I check on him or will that just make things worse?* I dropped the kids off at the bowling alley, grateful that they were finally old enough I didn't have to go with them. I set out for a walk, hopefully two games of bowling long. Already at 10:00 in the morning it was hot and humid, more like mid-July than Memorial Day.

Climbing the hills as fast as I could, drenching in sweat that somehow rinses off grief, I began to focus on this world again. Where it was hot, not shivery cold. Looking into other people's yards as they got ready for their holiday cookouts, I imagined their families. *Those people look fine, but maybe everyone has an invisible frozen place inside them?*

I picked the kids up. When it started raining on our way home, the kids rolled down their windows and stuck their heads out for the cool breeze. It'd been a hot, dry spring; everyone was talking about the weather, worrying that this early heat would hurt the gardens. The rain brought relief, but there was something ominous with it—yellowish-green clouds tinged with deep, blue black towered up over the hills. We slowed down to stare, and without warning, a driving rain mixed with hail swept over us. Hail pounded down, bouncing on the road, as ice glazed over the windshield.

The roaring wind made it impossible to hear and I couldn't see. Afraid that stopping would be even more dangerous than driving, I reached my hand out the window and scratched a hole in the ice with my fingernails as we inched along to the general store. We slid into the parking lot, alongside other cars parked at strange angles, and joined a crowd huddled in the doorway. People stood, staring at the ice sweeping by.

A woman stumbled in, bleeding and crying, covered with shards of glass. A branch had shattered her windshield. A couple of people tore themselves away from the ferocious power of the storm to take care of her. Whimpering, Sophie clung to me, but I stood still, patting her absently, mesmerized.

The kids finally dragged me from the doorway into the store so we could buy supplies for our cookout, which would be inside this year. After the storm blew by, we inched home without snow tires through the sudden midwinter landscape.

When we got home, a wildly excited big brother greeted us, "Hey, did you see that awesome storm?" Noah wanted to show us all the places hail had collected, driven into piles by the fierce wind. He tore off his shoes to stand in a small mountain of hail on the deck, striking a pose, so I would take a photograph to document the moment. Then the kids turned on the TV to see if there was anything about the storm on the weather channel, and I went outside to investigate.

That's when I saw it, my new garden that I'd been tending all spring. It had grown back this year full and lush with perennials. I had just built a rock border and added annuals for color. This was my welcome garden that greeted you when you came to my door.

And it was buried in ice. Fledgling baby annuals with their brave flowers lay tattered on the ground. The tops of the taller perennials were snapped off, or left hanging like broken arms. Plants that had been blooming just hours before were in deep freeze.

Dropping to my knees I started scooping ice away, using fingernails to snip off broken stalks and throwing them in a heap. I picked off the shredded flowers and threw them onto the pile.

But it was impossible to get all the ice off without causing more damage. After a while I just gave up, and went inside to warm my hands which didn't work. They needed time and attention before they could be put to use again.

Maybe it's still early enough in the growing season for the plants to repair themselves? This had never happened to me before, and I wasn't an experienced enough gardener to know for sure.

But it wasn't just the sudden ice storm or the garden—of course, it never is. A nightmare with elements of both taunted me all night, scenes of a garden so full of life, now ruined; that little girl, huddled against the cold, eyes wild, frantically searching. I finally drifted off early in the morning, dreaming the dream prayer that we would have enough time left in our own season.

10

The Grocery Store

SOMETIMES WHEN PEOPLE FINISH reading one of my stories they pause, and say, "Well, I liked it. But what's it *about*?" And I say, "Lots of things." But I'll tell you from the beginning that this story isn't about what happened to Sophie when she was five that's left her feeling timid, not as brave as she used to be when she was four-and-a-half. Now she's afraid to do things other eight-year-olds can handle without any problem. I'm thinking about this as we pull up to the gym for her swim team practice. I have some shopping to do, and it would be so much easier if I could just drop her off, and watch her walk in, making sure she gets though the heavy front doors safely, without having to find a parking space. Then I could go to the store, and still be back in time to watch her swim laps, back and forth, back and forth. (It's a sign of my great devotion that I sit there at all, because as soon as I hit the humidity, I have a hot flash.) But she needs me to watch her and so I suffer through it, the boring repetition and the heat, reminding myself that being a mother is filled with difficult moments. And this one doesn't begin to qualify.

We pull over to the curb. "Can you go in by yourself? I'll be right back." Amazingly, she agrees to try, and standing straight she looks proud marching off, a small solitary figure heading for the heavy front door. Then I'm off, on my way to the store.

I like this store a lot. It's not too big, so I don't get overwhelmed, and it's filled with beautiful fruits and vegetables and all sorts of interesting ethnic foods, some I don't even recognize. The aesthetics of the food: how it's displayed, the colors, the freshness, it's all part of what I need to have a delightful, pre-swim practice shopping experience.

In the lobby, surrounded by empty carts, I realize I've forgotten my shopping list. I'm usually organized so this is a rare occurrence. Now here I am stuck trying to remember what the kids *must* have to feel they're being adequately provided for. (Which, of course, is different for each of them; there is almost no overlap.) The only area of agreement seems to be Diet Coke which, I know, is filled with all sorts of nasty chemicals but, for some reason, we all like, and I buy it religiously, against my better judgment.

Let's see: the special things I've come here for today are matzo, gefilte fish, and horseradish root. Passover starts in a couple of days and we're making our annual effort to observe the holiday. The Seder carries added significance for me because we never had one when I was growing up. I've had to learn the ritual along with how to "cook Jewish." No one but me eats the gefilte fish, but we all like matzo. We only observe one or two days of the traditional eight so we need other groceries: Frosted Cheerios for Sophie, Grapenuts for Noah who's on a health-kick, spelt cereal for me. I'm trying to reduce the amount of wheat I eat. The kids think this is funny and can't resist saying things like, "Spelt cereal. *Spelt?* How's it spelt?" and then laughing hysterically.

I leave the cart as I retrace my steps to pick up some things I've forgotten. On the way back, I round the corner and have a momentary lapse, standing there. Blank. *Where did I put my cart? Oh, there it is,* with the beat-up old canvas sacks I bring so I don't use brown paper bags. I know it doesn't make any difference in the grand scheme of things, but it makes me feel like I'm doing my little bit, using up fewer trees in the world.

The Grocery Store

I pass the towering pyramid of Passover foods displayed prominently in the center of the store. *As if there were enough Jews in our town to buy all that matzo,* as I grab my two boxes and push on. I'm almost done, moving toward my favorite part of the store, the bulk food section.

This makes me feel virtuous, too, because I'm using less packaging. I'm standing there scanning the rows of spices trying to remember what I need. *Oh, yeah, curry.* I put several scoops in a little plastic bag, label it CURRY, so I don't mix it up with other spices at home. *Good, now I'm done, I'll get back to the pool with plenty of time to spare.*

As I wheel toward the front of the store, I hear someone complaining in a loud voice, heavy with a German accent. Rounding the corner I see an old woman, tall, broad shoulders, standing very erect. She's talking to one of the young clerks who's cowering under the barrage of words. I can see he's trying to help her with something. *What's her problem? Not my business,* I remind myself, pushing my cart up the aisle toward the checkout line.

And then, abruptly, out of the corner of my eye, I see it. All of the old canvas bags that I bring with me are dirty, off-white—*oh God*—there's one blue *bag sitting right there in the cart I'm pushing. I don't own any blue canvas bags. What's that doing there?*

Instantaneously, it becomes clear to me what's going on, and without thinking, I grab all my groceries that I can hold in one hand and sneak down the aisle away from the complaining woman. I take the important things I can carry without looking suspicious: the curry, spelt cereal, horseradish root and the matzo. (No one will miss the gefilte fish.) But I can't pick up the Diet Coke, the 24 CAN BOX! is too heavy. I say a furtive goodbye to it as I abandon it.

Walking briskly down the aisle, I practically bump into my real cart, waiting right where I left it. Depositing my rescued purchases, I wheel away acting like I've had this cart all along.

But she spied me, that tall, erect old woman, and I sense her coming, bearing down on me, striding fast, her eyes searching me out. The voice, the accent, how swiftly she's coming . . . In an instant I'm not me anymore. (You know how sometimes people will do something, and then afterwards they'll say, "I don't know what happened, that's just *not me*"?) It's like I've fallen through a portal. Where am I?

Caught.

How bad is it, what I've done? Can I deny it, pretend it was someone else? Should I run away? Quick, look, is there anyplace to hide?

"I think," she begins, her voice guttural and accusing, "you have put your things in my cart."

The cowering not-me who planned to hide, or at least lie, is forcefully banished as I pull myself back to the present, become the adult I am. "Yes, my mistake," I murmur. "I guess you don't really want these things," pointing to the Diet Coke mega box, the Frosted Cheerios, the artificial chocolate drink boxes. Trying to be light-hearted.

"No, I don't," A disdainful bark. She's glaring, watching me vigilantly to make sure I take everything out.

What now? How do I escape with any shred of self-esteem, a mother who feeds her kids that kind of food, and mixes up carts? And, even worse, thinks about running away. I know, maybe I just won't tell anyone about what happened to me at the store today. It'll be a secret to add to the others, big and small, that I've collected over the years.

I make it back to the pool in plenty of time to sit in the bleachers and sweat. I watch Sophie swim her laps, and wonder what the hell that portal business was all about, but this private questioning is interrupted because she's climbing the concrete steps, dripping pool water, smiling up at me.

Toweling Sophie off I change my mind about my new secret. I start telling her the story about the old woman and the mixed-up shopping carts, embellishing it, making it funnier. But I leave out the detail about falling through a hole and turning into the terrified *not-me* who wanted to run away.

She laughs and takes my hand, because she thinks I'm being so silly. We walk to the car holding hands, all three of us.

Hard Listening

11

What I Heard

WHEN WE'D MOVED EAST to be near my mother, I spent the first four months interviewing for jobs in a town saturated with social workers. I finally found a position at the Peter Bent Brigham Hospital, even though I'd never worked in a hospital before. I was in my late twenties then, on a career fast track, I hadn't had Noah yet—hadn't even thought of it. There was so much to learn, my new boss had never been one for coddling people. She assigned me to the Burn Unit, and the ICU; I taught medical students a class on interviewing. Work dominated my life, demanding all my time and creative energy. I had to stay focused or I would never get everything done. I couldn't afford to procrastinate, no "down-to-the-wire" for me, which actually suited me fine, because I'd always hated how procrastinating made me feel. I planned out my day with a detailed schedule—Ms. Hyper-Organized, colleagues called me—to make sure I'd keep plugging away, and get everything finished ahead of time. I'd done this in college and graduate school. I even did it when it was my turn to do housework or grocery shopping. Lists, outlines, flow charts: that was me. It's not that I'm all that virtuous by nature; it's just that having things hanging over my head makes me anxious. Better to get something done than deal with the anxiety of *not* having done it.

That's the way I talked to myself. *Don't put things off, it just gets you in trouble.* I was a real NIKE girl, of the JUST-DO-IT variety.

The one time I did put something off, it turned out that, even without any prior experience, I was an expert procrastinator.

Here's what happened: When I was twenty-nine I had a conversation that could have changed my life. One brittle November day my friend Rachel and I spent our lunch break walking around the Medical School quad. It required numerous laps around the yard to get any exercise, but we had an hour and as we strode, we talked. Rachel was a new friend, and I listened carefully to everything she said. Since I was a professional listener, I knew how to pay attention to tone and nuance, I was experienced in trying to make sense of what I heard. That day I was particularly intrigued because she told me two things I had never heard anyone say before. She told me, "I feel like a frog," at the beginning of the hour and, as we were parting, "I'm like a horse being led into a furnace."

I didn't say much. I nodded, making appropriately concerned noises. Then I spent the rest of the day puzzling over Rachel's disclosures. "I feel like a frog," meaning, "I see myself jumping from topic to topic"? That worked. But what about the "horse being led into a furnace"? *This is enigmatic and kind of horrific, an unconscious reference to the Holocaust perhaps?* I couldn't be sure, and since I was professionally trained, I tried not to jump to conclusions. I called Rachel the next day to check on her emotional state.

She was fine. She did wonder why I seemed so concerned, but I wasn't prepared to talk about it yet. I was just relieved she was okay and besides I had something of my own to deal with. I wasn't ready to tell her. Or even myself.

By the time we knew each other better I found out what she really meant: "I feel like a frog" meant "I feel like a fraud," and the horse was just a horse, but that "furnace" was really a harness. Everything slipped back into place. Nothing to worry about.

As time went by, Rachel and I drifted apart. Only the funny story about the horse in the furnace remained of our friendship.

Then, a year or so later, I was talking on the phone to Isaac, cradling it on my left shoulder like I always do. Squeezing the phone to my ear, I realized he was whispering. *Why is he doing that? Is he telling me a secret or something or is there someone on his end of the line he doesn't want to overhear?* When I asked him to speak louder, he didn't. *Geez, that is so aggravating that someone I'm close to, my own brother, would ignore me like that.* But what could I do? I just let it go.

But when *everyone* I talked to on the phone started whispering, I got so fed up with straining to understand, that I had to do something. A lifelong habit is hard to break, but I made myself try. I changed telephone ears.

And I could hear. Perfectly.

That's when I first went to the doctor. "What's happening to me?" I asked. "Everyone's whispering into my left ear, but I can hear just fine with my right." Maybe the diagnosis should have been obvious, but you can see I was confused about what was wrong. That day I had my first hearing exam. And found out I was almost completely deaf in my left ear.

"Have you been pregnant recently?" the young doctor asked.

Well, no, I wanted to snap at him. *Could he tell by looking in my ears that I was a lesbian trying to conceive, with little success? No, of course not.* "Why?"

"Because what you have—otoschlerosis—often follows pregnancy in young women like you. We don't know why."

I had just turned thirty. No one in my family had ever been deaf; even my Grandma Crystal, who lived to the impressive age of ninety-three, died with perfect hearing.

The doctor explained that a hearing aid would probably be helpful, but it would amplify *all* sound, leaving me in a loud world where I wouldn't be able to distinguish the important from the irrelevant. Surgery was an option, but the surgeon could not guarantee success and vertigo was a possible side effect. I didn't need dizziness along with my maybe-not-restored hearing. *No, thanks.*

So I went back to hearing what I could; sound—faint noises wrapped in cotton batting, traveling over a distance—finally arrived at their destination, my ears. Like traffic after a heavy snowfall, the sounds that reached me were soft, muffled. Not a terrible problem to have, really. And, in fact, I discovered that diminished hearing had some positive aspects: I could turn down the volume on distracting noises at night by sleeping with my bad ear up. I could minimize the amount of chatter I had to endure at parties by turning my left ear to people who bored me. I'd become the living incarnation of the phrase *to turn a deaf ear.*

Other, even more significant changes over the coming years required adjustments, too. I just added coping with the new way the world sounded to the list. Ruth and I moved to Vermont, Noah was born, then Ruth and I separated, my mother who'd just been sick, was now dying. Amid all these changes, I decided to add one more and open my own therapy practice. My hearing seemed to have stabilized. I could hear Noah if he cried out at night. And I could hear my clients just fine. While jokes about what I *thought* I'd heard became commonplace, I found I could live with hearing most of what went on around me because, after all, who needed to absorb *everything*? The best way to cope was to consider it a minor inconvenience, an amusing aspect of my new life.

Later Sophie was born, and when she was old enough to join Noah in playing tricks, their favorite game became calling out "Mommy!" in a restaurant while they watched me turn circles trying to locate them. If I was looking for them in the house, calling, "Sophie? Where are you? Noah?" they giggled, calling back, "Here!"—tittering while I searched. "Here" meant nothing to me.

I got used to swiveling my head, if I wanted to hear what the person on my left was saying. Awkward, but tolerable. I got used to explaining to people that if I didn't answer when they spoke to me, I wasn't ignoring them, I just couldn't hear. It didn't seem to bother anyone else.

But after I'd been in practice for several years I noticed some shift, an increased silence in my office. *What's happening now?* Listening the way a therapist listens had become difficult. At first I thought I was just tired, that working full time, taking care of the kids by myself, was wearing me down. And that could have been it. So I took a vacation. But even though I returned refreshed, with renewed energy and enthusiasm for work, something still wasn't right. Listening and talking, the tools of therapy, had become burdensome. Suddenly, it seemed everything my clients said frustrated me. Like the vacation had never happened.

I was a professional listener. I loved my work. This is what I *did*, this was who I *was*. And yet the simple act of listening itself was turning into work. My hearing stopped being a joke, and turned into a real worry. Now sometimes I had to strain to really understand what a client was saying if they mumbled or looked away when they talked.

That's when I had to face facts: I'd started to rely on being able to see someone's mouth. I was lipreading.

Nothing showed, no limp, scar, or bruise to give me away. I still looked young, so unless I said something about my hearing loss people assumed I could hear just like they could. And even when I said I was "half-deaf," the easiest way to describe it, the fact didn't seem to register. Because everyone continued to talk at their normal volume. Normal for them, which was almost impossible for me. I took to smiling and nodding in agreement, even when I didn't know what I was agreeing to.

And then the logging trucks came. The small Vermont village I live in doesn't have much traffic, which is part of its appeal. Except for logging trucks, which seemed to appear suddenly, a new problem. But, of course, they'd been there all along, I'd just never noticed how they barreled down Main Street, shifting gears, drowning out sound, until a background of absolute silence became essential to my work. At first the trucks were a distraction, but as time went on they became an insurmountable obstacle. Because when they rumbled by I couldn't hear anything—not one word—of what my clients were saying.

Why was it so hard to get help? Why was I so secretive? I wonder that now. Because in the past I'd taken a certain pride myself in knowing when I needed to. Being able to ask for help is a *strength*, not a weakness, I often assured my clients. (Another example of advice that's easy to give, but not so easy to follow.)

But somehow this felt different. I was invested in people not learning something that was true about me. I was "passing," acting *as if* I were just like everyone else. Which was a lie. The truth was I didn't want to live with the changes that facing my new reality would bring. Listening—my connection to other people, the key to my livelihood—had failed me. The truth was that I was beginning to drift into my own, ever-quieter world. And, in that quiet, miraculously, I could hear whispers from the past perfectly: things I wished I had said during arguments long over, conversations with my dead mother, the night murmurs my babies had made while they slept. There was something appealing, seductive even, about that hushed realm. No struggle to hear, no need to respond. Just deepening silence.

I was drifting off into that silence, comforted by sounds of a familiar past. In spite of its appeal, though, my kids—always my best teachers—made it clear that I had to stay in the present. So I quit. I said goodbye to my clients, closed the practice. I wasn't a therapist anymore.

Which left the question: *What next? I'm only forty-eight, I should have lots of years left to do exciting, challenging work. What can I do? Who can I be?* All I knew for sure was that whatever I chose couldn't depend on listening.

Like many women of my generation I had been stretched, almost to breaking, by the demands of working while raising my children. *I'm a single mother, and who knows if that will ever change. Maybe I could consider this as an opportunity to be a stay-at-home mom, devoting myself to my kids. Good mothering can be fulfilling, a full-time occupation*, I assured myself. *But will there be enough money from the family business for me to take early retirement?*

Once I stopped seeing clients, almost without missing a beat, I started my new full-time job, carting the kids from one activity to the next, attending school conferences, cheering at swim meets, carpooling from play rehearsals. The whirlwind of the kids' lives caught me up, and wouldn't set me down. And without the requirement that I listen to other people's problems, I was free to focus entirely on them. While before Noah and Sophie might have complained that I didn't always pay enough attention to them, now they got a dose of what full-time attention meant. Noah was a junior in high school, starting to have his own life, and he, in his infinite teenage wisdom, had some advice. "Mom," he said, "I think you need to find work. You can't make Sophie and me your full-time job."

But there was still plenty to think about: Sophie was in seventh grade, dealing with the trials of middle school. Noah had college visits and applications ahead of him. But it soon became obvious that Noah was right, that making your kids into a full-time job has its downside: too much attention can backfire. Turns out you can care *too* much whether they get their homework in on time, whether they have a date for the junior prom.

I was still pondering this new reality, how to live my own life alongside the frenetic busyness of the kids' lives, how to take care of them without caring *too much*, what kind of *real* job I should look for. While I was taking my time, a moment—one of those moments that forces changes in your life that you're really not prepared for—required me to review that decision made years before, that I would live with my less-than-perfect hearing.

I heard something that changed everything: early one morning on a school day, I was taking a shower when twelve-year-old Sophie knocked on the door, asking if she could come in to brush her teeth. I shouted over the splashing water, "What are you doing after school?"

She paused, as if considering, and then answered, "The coleslaw is a heavy burden."

What?

"The coleslaw is a heavy burden?" I shouted, incredulous.

She doubled over, choking she was laughing so hard. "Mom, you are too much, I can't wait to get to school to tell my friends!" I laughed along with her. I mean, it *was* pretty funny.

But what if she'd said, "I'm going over to Cindy's house to snort coke," or, "I've decided I'm ready to have sex with Peter"?

So after she'd left for school, and I was alone, I had a serious talk with myself. *That's it*, I said. *This has gone on long enough. You claim that you hate procrastinating, but this has been going on— how long now?—almost twenty years. That's it.*

And that *was* it.

I made an appointment for a hearing exam.

They'll just tell me what I already know, that I can't hear out of my left ear. I'll ask if hearing aids have improved over the years. If not, and if surgery is the only option that really works, I'll do it.

The appointment wasn't for another week, which left lots of time to remember all the things I've *misheard*. What I didn't know was what I'd missed. What's been going on in the world around me that I didn't hear as I'd been sliding into a silent cocoon?

I guess it's time to rejoin the noisy world. One thing will be different, that's for sure: there would be no more horses in the furnace, no more coleslaw that's a heavy burden.

12

Fire

CARLA CALLED AT 6:30 in the morning. Usually we have our morning conversation at 8:00 so I knew something was up. "Jesse, I just read the obituary of a young woman from Greenfield. Really young. It mentioned her partner, so I wondered if she was gay and if you knew her."

Oh, no—this snippet of information was just enough to make me afraid I did know who she was talking about. I was already conjuring up faces. "Who did you say it was again?" She repeated the name, and it was the people I'd imagined: the Susan who had just died, and Susan, her lover, who had been the very first clients I saw when I opened my private practice. They came together for couples' counseling; after I'd seen them together, one of the Susans came on her own. They were young then, but had already been together a long time, long enough to have "issues" to sort through to decide if they wanted to stay together. The irony wasn't wasted on me that as we delved into their emotional struggles, I was making that terrible drive over the mountains to visit my dying mother. Each week I saw them, my mother was worse. Focusing on "the Susans"—as they called themselves—and their problems was a relief. Sometimes I wondered if *I* should be paying *them*, I was so grateful for the change of focus.

When Susan died last week she had just celebrated her thirty-ninth birthday. I remember her as the livelier of the two, dramatic and effusive, a young woman with life force pulsing, somehow trapped inside, on the verge of exploding, dying to be released. But she couldn't allow herself to let loose. I blamed myself for not knowing how to make it safe enough for her to express all that teeming vitality. But in spite of what we weren't able to do together, we still did a lot and parted with mutual respect, even as we both sensed something essential was left undone.

I knew I had go to the funeral, even though I wouldn't know anyone, except the surviving Susan. At the church, sitting next to a stranger, it was a consolation to hear her friends describe all that pent-up vitality that she had somehow, somewhere, found a way to harness. (Therapy is only one way, and it doesn't work for everyone.) Susan had discovered another path, and grown more and more into herself, a teacher and a healer. Friends called her a shaman in describing how she'd helped them.

The service was long; many people spoke, there was lots of time for silent reflection, and for full-throated singing. Listening to Susan's friends remembering her something shifted inside me, and the worry that I had failed her released its grip. We'd walked as far as we could together, because by the time we said goodbye we recognized that we spoke different languages—mine the language of psychology, hers the language of the soul, and the struggle to translate had become just that, a struggle. Thankfully, we parted before we drove each other crazy.

Now, these many years later, as I wrestle with my own spiritual journey, begun when I visited the psychic, Vincent, deepened by my work with Dorothy, I was just starting to reach that place where Susan lived. I could use *her* help now.

Looking towards the front pew where the surviving Susan sat with the family, I imagined as best I could living her shock and fresh grief. I stared at the back of her head and noticed—*gray, gray?*—how her hair had turned. Her composure, so different from the anxious energy of her younger self, as she stood next to Susan's father while he spoke about his dead daughter, his voice infused with tears: "I promised myself I would not weep."

I wanted to say something to Susan, but I couldn't face the reception. Too many people, too much talking. I left a card. *It seems so cliché-filled, but what do you say that doesn't sound like a cliché?* and walked out of the church, standing for a moment on the stairs, in the too-bright afternoon. Not quite ready to leave, gazing at all the people exiting the church—*I was right, I don't know anyone*—and there on the sidewalk, there was Susan, greeting people, hugging, saying, "Thank you for coming." I joined a crowd waiting to speak to her.

And then, my turn. There we stood facing one another, me remembering the very young woman I'd known, gazing into the eyes of the middle-aged woman she had become. She said, "Jesse," and I, with all my expertise in words, couldn't say anything except, "Oh, Susan." We hugged, held each other, swaying. She said, "Thank you for coming." *I'll call you,* I thought as I turned away.

I went home to an empty house in the middle of that hot afternoon and climbed into bed, lying very, very still, until it was obvious that sleep would not rescue me. I was concentrating hard on remembering details about Susan's life, about her family, her relationships with those brothers and sisters I'd just heard reminiscing. About her father, that old man, fumbling to remember what he wanted to say, trying so desperately not to cry. I wanted to recall her story—that her mother had died young, that she was the youngest of seven—the way I had heard it so many years before.

Suddenly: *I know what I can do. I can look through the files to help me remember.* I'd kept the records from when I was a therapist, pages and pages of notes about each person I saw over the years, still stored in the garage, waiting for me to decide what to do with them. Those cabinets took up a lot of space, but I'd gotten stalled trying to figure out how to get rid of them. I'm sure I could've solved the problem, but a thornier question kept me stuck: what would it signify if I did? Did those files mean I might still be a therapist, that I could go back to my office some day and resume the only profession I'd ever known?

And if I could release myself from my own past enough to make a plan, how should I dispose of them in a way that worked *and* was respectful?

Now, suddenly, the answer was obvious.

Fire.

In our family, fire is revered. No one but me knows the depth of the ice build-up inside. They just know that for us, heat is essential. As winter eclipsed fall and the dark days descended, we seized any excuse to celebrate with food and light; we always had a bonfire for Hannukah and, of course, the Solstice. Anna is the fire-maker in our family, but this was something I needed to do, in my own way, alone. At the fire circle at the edge of the yard, I stared down into charred wood and ashes from past fires, and yes, it seemed right.

Carrying as many files as I could, I dropped them into the charred pile. One spilled open and I paused to scan the pages—and, without anticipating it, I was face to face with a particular client—staring straight into the past where her face crumpled when she cried, hearing what she whispered about her mother, her lover, her brother. I murmured a quick goodbye, because there wouldn't be time for a lengthy visitation with nine file boxes overflowing with individual stories. I crumpled the pages, lighting them carefully to make sure the fire would catch, scattering them one-by-one into the flames.

Burning took hours. Smoke drifted into the night sky. Soot clung to my skin where the ashes and smoke touched me.

Somehow the long burning in the summer heat purified. I'd needed to finish with that part of my life, but I hadn't known how much until that moment. By now most of the paper had turned to ash, and I was tired and ready to stop. I'd been working my way through the files, most of the pages were smoldering, but I hadn't reached Susan yet. Looking for her was, after all, what got me started in the first place.

I flipped through a cabinet until I found Susan's file, but inside the folder was empty. *Oh, damn, I must have filed her sessions under the other Susan's name* as I tossed the empty folder into the flames.

Later when I got to the last drawer—*It's got to be here*—and it was, the living Susan's file. I said her name aloud as I began to read. Inside was a complete record describing her. But not one word about the Susans as a couple, and no notes about the dead Susan. *What did I do with them?* Whatever memories I had would have to do.

The fire burned and burned. When it was over, all that was left was an enormous pile of blackened and smoldering paper. In the dark I could see that I had burned up part of my past. And something had melted inside.

After I said goodbye to my clients and closed the practice, I had thought of myself as a former-therapist, and all those people I'd seen I called former-clients. Those were the categories I used. It's not easy to change how you understand your own history, the labels you use to organize yourself in relation to the rest of the world, but I need to. Because those categories are meaningless now. And they keep me stuck in the past tense.

I just want to be the person Susan greeted in front of the church: "Oh, Jesse, thank you for coming."

Right Work

13

Vincent

*B*ACK WHEN I WAS thirty-nine—with forty looming like roiling thunderclouds on the horizon—I began acting like I was smack in the throes of a mid-life crisis. Clichéd as it sounds these fifteen long years later—forty sounds young to me now—but then I felt like I didn't have a choice, forty was bearing down on me, and *I had to do something.*

Time for some straight talk: *Face facts, Jesse. How you've been living life so far hasn't been all that successful. The new year is here;* 1990, *a new decade, time to try something new.*

Time to leave my house on Romance Lane in New Canaan, to go all the way to New York for an appointment with Vincent, a well-known psychic (well-known, that is, to people who know such things), so famous he didn't even need a last name. Just Vincent to those of us in the know. I'd heard about him from Carla who'd consulted him twice, and who, in spite of deep-seated skepticism, reported she was "stunned" by her encounters with him. High praise from Carla. No generic palm-reading, you-will-fall-in-love-with-a-tall-dark-stranger here.

"Vincent has the uncanny ability to see immediately, without preamble, into the heart of everything." Because I trusted Carla, and because I felt the need to crack out of my usual mode, I decided to write for an appointment, not mentioning anything except who referred me. Since Vincent had a long waiting list it'd take several months to hear back, and longer before I'd have to decide if I'd really go through with it. *Good going, Jesse. You've done something, but you haven't really committed yourself, you can always back out.*

Just ten days later, to my surprise, I got a letter for an appointment. *Oh, no, now what?* My cynical self had a long argument with the part that wanted to experiment, try new things. Eventually the parts negotiated a compromise: I'd go for the appointment but maintain my attitude of I-don't-believe-any-of-this-stuff-but-I'll-just-check-it-out-anyway. By happy coincidence my brother, Ben, lived in the same town where Vincent had his office, so I could stay at his house and go for the appointment in the morning. If the session with Vincent turned out to be New Age drivel I'd have someone to laugh about it with. I was already working up some funny lines about being psyched out.

Arrangements had to be made. Baby Sophie was just six months old; she could stay with her regular babysitter, but how would I get to New York and what should I do with Noah? It was my weekend with him. Usually he was with Ruth on weekends, but this was my once-a-month weekend and we always tried to do something special. When I told Noah I'd be taking the train to visit Uncle Ben, he begged to come along, since he'd never taken a train before. So that was the special part.

But what would he do during my session with Vincent? There wasn't anyone to babysit, so he'd have to come with me. I assumed this wouldn't be a problem since Noah was a precocious little boy, an early reader. He could read a book, or take a nap in the waiting room. My sessions with clients only lasted fifty minutes or an hour at most. I assumed the session would be the same. Noah and I talked it over, and he assured me he could wait that long.

Everything was falling into place.

The novelty of being on the train wore off quickly for me, but Noah was thrilled with every minute of our six-hour adventure. He loved everything: the towns whizzing by, the chairs that tipped back, the conductor who collected our tickets and took a special interest in him, and the bad food in the dining car that we carried in a cardboard tray, swaying, trying not to drop anything onto the laps of our fellow passengers.

When Ben picked us up at the train station it was late, way past Noah's bedtime. That was a thrill, too.

We took a cab to the office the next morning. When Vincent met us at the door, I could barely concentrate on his greeting, I was so mesmerized by his appearance. *Why didn't Carla warn me?* Vincent didn't look like any man I'd ever seen. He stood well over six feet tall, his black hair like a thick rug on his huge head, with penetrating eyes as black as his hair. In spite of his size there was something distinctly female in his demeanor. He wasn't effeminate, in any usual sense, but he had a kind of womanliness about him that was hard to locate. This impression grew stronger as he took my hand in both of his enormous hands, enveloping me in softness, and drew me into the apartment. I knew that I was in the presence of someone who was fully himself, equal parts man and woman.

I didn't have time to sort it all out because now Noah and I were standing awkwardly in the waiting room. And what a room it was, like my favorite antique stores, overfilled with ornately carved mahogany chairs and brocade-covered couches. Towering bookcases with leaded-glass doors crammed with leather-bound books lined the perimeter of the enormous parlor. There was a display case with Victorian porcelain dolls, each dressed in miniature, historically accurate costumes. Fragile artifacts were artfully arranged on every conceivable surface. You expected a warning, a DO NOT TOUCH sign. Every piece in the entire room looked priceless. And breakable.

If I didn't know better I'd have thought we'd wandered onto the set of some old horror film. While Noah and I stood taking it all in, Vincent, perhaps sensing that we were overwhelmed, offered an explanation: "Oh, this was my dead parents' apartment," as if that said everything.

I couldn't tell if I was more worried about leaving my five-year-old in the cavernous room or about the safety of the precious artifacts. I stood, wondering what it'd be like for Noah to wait here, when I got another surprise. "Our appointment will be only two hours," Vincent assured me, his soft voice musical, soothing. As I glanced over at Noah, I saw worry flicker across his face, and realized I'd better play to the part of him that always wanted to act grown-up. "Sit here," I whispered, as I escorted him to the Victorian couch covered in faded maroon velvet. "You'll be fine here," I patted the formal couch trying to make it look inviting. "You can read." I kissed him on the head as he picked up his book. "You'll be fine. I'll be back before you know it."

I followed Vincent down the narrow hallway to his consulting room, kicking myself. *What whim had led me here to talk to this, this person of indeterminate gender, who doesn't know anything about my life? What could he possibly have to say to me?*

As I sat down in a worn rocking chair Vincent began fiddling with an elaborate taping system, checking and double-checking equipment. The longer he fussed, the more intimidated, and then fidgety, I became. After several minutes sitting, worrying about how much time this would add to Noah's wait, I dared suggest, "It's fine not to tape the session. Can we get started?"

"You won't be able to remember everything," he declared with the certainty of someone with whom you do not argue. "You'll be glad later that you have the tape."

I'd come this far. There was no choice but to take his word for it.

Vincent did tell me many things. He started by reviewing my past lives: one as a courtesan in ancient Persia, another as a goatherd in the mountains of Spain. My favorite was when I was the son of a French duke, a student of neuroscience, before the time of Sigmund Freud. Being a therapist myself, I was delighted to hear my work had pre-dated Freud. I asked so many questions about these past lives that we ran out of time. Vincent suggested that I come for another session to focus our attention on my future. I'd been in a crisis about my career. And my love life. Maybe Vincent could help me find my way.

"Let me tell you something," he said. "I don't usually offer advice but I feel like I have to say this... don't bother trying to develop your fine motor skills. No amount of effort will turn you into someone who's good at hand work. So don't consider moving to the mountains in Colorado to take up knitting or needlepoint."

Is he kidding? Of course, I'm not going to move or take up needlepoint, but how did he know that my disinterest in hand work was one of the few things my knitting mother and I had ever argued about?

I had to ask a final question, not about me, but about the kids. Because I wasn't sure I ever would come back. He'd already met Noah and I pulled a photo of Sophie out of my wallet. What did the future hold for them?

Vincent was definite: Noah would be a scientist and Sophie a dancer. I wanted to squeeze in one last question about me—what might *I* become?—but I'd waited too long. I'd spent my time learning about who I'd been. Our time was up. We sat for a quiet minute together. I don't know about Vincent, but I was trying to absorb some of his essence, his calming certainty. Then he leaned forward, taking my hand in both of his. I felt that softness envelop me again, as he stared into my eyes. Then, cocking his head as if listening to something, he murmured, "You will write in spite of yourself."

With that he stood up, clicked off the tape recorder, and handed me two tapes. Our consultation was over.

Vincent held the door open for me. Stepping into the hallway, I nearly stumbled over Noah leaning against the wall beside the door, asleep. I guess the waiting room got to be too much for him, after all. Ruffling his hair to wake him, we followed Vincent back to the waiting room where he shook hands solemnly, first with Noah, then me, as we said goodbye.

Back home I was eager to play the tapes, because Vincent had been right, I didn't remember everything. I wanted to listen to the whole session again, curious about what I might have missed. Even if I couldn't bring myself to actually believe what Vincent said, it had certainly been captivating. But when I pressed PLAY, you could only make out a faint drone of voices beneath the buzz of static. I couldn't hear a single word.

A friend of a friend was a sound engineer; he was confident that he could clean the tapes, find the words. But after he'd tinkered for hours, you still couldn't really hear anything. Just louder buzzing.

Still I refused to give up. I was determined to hear some—any part at all—of that session where I was introduced to who I'd been. I listened to the entire thing, all two hours' worth, fast-forwarding, stopping at regular intervals, desperately straining to capture at least a few of Vincent's pronouncements.

But after all that, there was only one sentence you could hear distinctly, the one at the very end, Vincent declaring, "You will write in spite of yourself."

14

Looking for Work

Vincent's pronouncement about me writing made me nervous, even more uncertain about my future than I'd been before I consulted him. So when I got a call from Mrs. Teeney, the secretary at Sophie's school, asking, "Would you be available on Thursday afternoon to be the crossing guard?" I thought: *I guess I signed up to volunteer if the regular paid guard couldn't make it. This is news to me, but it must be true, I'm always forgetting things these days.* Since I retired I've been the back-up Meals-on-Wheels delivery person, why not be the temporary crossing guard?

"Sure," I said, "of course I'll do it. What time should I be there?" When I told Sophie and Noah about my new job, I did it like it was a joke, figuring teasing myself was the quickest way around being teased by them. Sophie thought it would be great fun to see her mom with a stop sign helping the little kids cross the street. Noah had been embarrassed when I retired so young and wanted me to get another job. He just rolled his eyes, letting the gesture speak for him.

Early Thursday morning, I got another call from the school. They wouldn't need me today, but could I come tomorrow? *Damn, I've been let go already, even before I've helped one first grader cross the street.* But, "Sure, I'll come Friday."

So Friday I went to the school early to collect my uniform, an orange vest and a big red STOP sign, from Mrs Teeney. I asked whether there was an orientation session or anything special I should know about my new job. She looked at me quizzically, not sure if I was kidding.

It was a late September day, still warm and breezy. I tried out my technique on little kids, the first graders. They seemed surprised to see a middle-aged, somewhat overweight woman clowning around with the STOP sign, but when I waved them across the street, they came willingly enough. And said, "Thank you."

I know lots of people in our small town. Many are former clients and they probably still think of me as their former therapist. But no one has ever known me as the crossing guard.

I had fun. Some of the kids grinned at my jokes when I deposited them safely on the other side. I told their parents that I had been looking for intellectually challenging work, and was glad to have found it. I escorted tiny kids—*are they old enough for school?*—and even big sixth graders who looked like they should be escorting me. I stopped some cars, and at least one logging truck. A man in my writing group drove by and hooted out the window.

I was outside on a beautiful morning. I had helped some kids feel safe. I greeted neighbors I hadn't seen for a while. I felt useful.

I'm glad I didn't get fired. Maybe that half-hour as the crossing guard is the end of that career, but I hope not. Meanwhile, to be on the safe side, I guess I should look for other work. But I'll be hoping each time the phone rings that they're calling me back so I get to put on my orange vest, pick up my STOP sign, and go stop traffic.

15

The Tiger's Eye

I'VE NEVER HAD ENOUGH time. Certainly not unscheduled, down time. Until I retired, that is. Now my life has changed so much that I hardly recognize it as mine. And it's so different from my friends' lives; everyone complains about how busy they are. Not me, I have too much free time. Well, it's not exactly free but at least it's unstructured, under my own control, that is, from 7:30 in the morning when I get the kids off to school till 3:00 when I pick them up. Then I'm on duty again for Debate Club meetings and swim team practice and school open houses and haircuts requiring driving, driving, driving. But since I retired when I was fifty, earlier than I'd ever imagined, I have unplanned-for time, seven and a half hours a day of it.

For the first time in my life.

Where did the time go before now? First, there was being a child in a family (lots of time, but none of it belonged to me) then school, college, work, then graduate school (including field placement, which is really work you don't get paid for), then a real, full-time paying job. The longest I'd had off before this was in the mid-'70s when Ruth and I packed up our house in Madison to move East. We took a six-week vacation, drove cross-country all the way to San Francisco, touched the Pacific and turned around, driving back to Boston.

Which is where I began a new lifestyle; the demanding life of the unemployed. You've heard about my job at the Brigham, but not about what it took to find that job. Every day for three months I put on my interview suit and went out looking for work in a town jammed-to-overflowing with social workers. Eighteen interviews later I was hired as director of social work at a hospital, the job that would define the next ten years of my life. Work was so challenging that immediately our cross-country drive and my unemployment faded into memory.

But back to my retirement: before I quit working, I wondered if all I'd do was lie on the couch and stare into space, not even able to appreciate the view out the sliding glass doors that led your eye to a view of the river with a backdrop of gently rolling hills. And that's exactly what happened. I languished there, collapsed, gazing inward, and wondered who I was becoming.

I cringed when people asked that innocent question, "What do you do?" Followed by, "But you don't look old enough to retire." I tried calling myself a housewife to see if that fit. It didn't. I had a house, but I'd never be a wife. Then I tried "homemaker" which wasn't much better. As anyone who's ever been a stay-at-home mother will tell you, taking care of home and children *is* a full-time job. Anyone who thinks it's easy, not really work at all, hasn't ever done it. Work without pay, job without status; it's hard to say you're a homemaker and feel proud.

It was during the second year of my retirement that I saw the tiger's eye again. What finally got me off the coach was a realization that grabbed a hold and wouldn't let go: I missed being connected to a world bigger than just my own—my kids, my dogs, my garden, my friends. My, my, my.

I tried volunteer work, joined committees at our synagogue, took courses. And I read, anything I could get my hands on. I picked up studying spiritual texts I had abandoned during my working life: Jewish mysticism, Buddhist philosophy, New Age healing. Sometimes I read more mundane material: newspapers, recipes, cereal boxes. I wasn't ready to read the Want Ads. Instead I made a list. First,

JOBS I COULD NEVER DO:
- Middle-School Math teacher (can't do math above 6th-grade level)
- Rock-climbing instructor (scared of heights)
- Zamboni driver (probably *could* be a zamboni driver but wouldn't enjoy making geometric patterns on ice at 4:30 a.m.)

Done with that, I came up with another.

JOBS I WOULD NEVER DO:
- Tollbooth ticket-taker (can't make change in my head fast enough, hate breathing car fumes, flat feet make standing all day impossible)
- International flight attendant (scared to fly, takes me forever to recover from jet-lag)
- Computer programmer (only just mastered e-mail)

Enough lists, back to reading. One morning drinking coffee, skimming the events section of the local college newspaper, skipping over the too esoteric topics, my eye settled on a talk with an intriguing title, "Women and the World Wide Web" to be given by a Johanna Szold-Rezak. I don't know anything about the Web, but I flatter myself that I do know a bit about women, so I began, naturally, to tell myself jokes about women and spiders and the tangled webs we weave. Once I finished entertaining myself, I focused on the speaker's name, which I recognized because who could forget a name like that? I remembered the woman it belonged to because she'd had been my client twenty-five years ago when she was an undergraduate at the University of Wisconsin and I was a neophyte therapist.

In every therapist's career there are one or two or maybe three clients who are extraordinary. By bringing you deep into their world, they capture your attention and won't let go. The most experienced psychiatrist I know described it: "They teach you it's okay to love." I learned that from Johanna.

We had stayed in touch for several years after we both left Madison, then over time and distance, our connection frayed. Now, she had reappeared to lecture on a subject any fourteen-year old would understand better than I would.

What synchronicity, Dorothy would have said. *What are you supposed to learn from this extraordinary opportunity to reconnect with her?*

I was mulling this over when I went to the lecture, leaving ten-year-old Sophie plunked in front of the television with a snack, promising I would be home in time to make dinner.

There was already a small crowd when I arrived at the lecture hall. Most of the people were vaguely familiar, young women I recognized from concerts or other lectures. The director of the Women's Center waved and came over. "Do you know the student presenting her final thesis today?"

Final thesis? What? Oh, I must be in the wrong room.

Excusing myself I went next door to the right room. Which was completely empty. Was I the only person who wanted to hear about women and the Web? *I'll wait a bit because I'm early.* I'm always fifteen minutes early. After sitting alone for a while I finally went to ask about the Szold-Rezak talk. That's when I found out I wasn't just fifteen *minutes* early, I was *one week and fifteen minutes* early.

A week later, I again left Sophie sitting in front of the TV with a snack, with the same promise to be home in time to make her supper. This time I felt vaguely anxious. *Will I be too early? Will Johanna recognize me? Will I recognize her? And what could we possibly have to say to each other after all these years?*

I had enough time to stop in town to get a cup of coffee before the lecture. On the sidewalk in front of the coffee shop I ran into my friend, Leni, with her new baby. I admired the baby who was propped on the hip of some woman whose back was to me, someone I'd never seen before, until she turned around. Then throwing her free arm around me, "Jesse! I'd know you anywhere."

Here was Johanna, twenty-five years older, but entirely recognizable, out taking a walk with Leni (they were friends from graduate school), doing the same mundane thing I was, buying a cup of coffee before a lecture.

Johanna, Leni, the baby and I strolled over to the lecture room, where I sat, enchanted, as I listened to Johanna's talk, not understanding much, but marveling at how grown-up and competent she was. Musing about the passage of time. After final questions and applause, I joined the line of admirers who shook Johanna's hand, thanking her. Reluctant to say goodbye, I asked, "What are you doing now?"

"We're having dinner with colleagues from the Women's Studies department. Would you like to come?"

"Great, but can I bring my kids?"

"Of course."

On the way home to pick up Sophie and Noah, it hit me—I had something to show Johanna, if I could remember where I'd put it.

Twenty-five years ago, the last time I'd seen Johanna, she'd given me a gift, a necklace she'd made in her Jewelry 101 class, a hand-polished stone set in sterling silver. The stone appeared deep green on first glance, then changed color when tilted into light, streaks of gold and blueblack winking, reflecting sunlight. A tiger's eye.

I had saved it all these years, storing it for safe keeping in a special place.

Sentimental by nature, I have many special treasures. I searched in the small onyx bowl that holds my collection of buttons, sea glass, and polished pebbles, and there it was. I slipped the tiger's eye in my pocket, and the kids and I drove to the restaurant.

I introduced the kids, then sat down between Johanna and Sophie. Everyone was busy studying their menus, Noah was busy answering questions about the Web, when I turned to Johanna. "I have something to show you. Here, do you remember this?" I held the tiger's eye up to the light and then placed it in her hand.

We both stared into the heart of the stone, which winked back in the light. "Of course," she said, quietly. "You helped me grow up. Are you still a therapist?"

"Well, no, I've retired. I'm looking for work. I want to write, but I'm scared I'll never be able to do it. I don't know how to begin."

"Listen, Jesse, the Web is just a side-line for me," she said. "I teach writing at Columbia. Send me something you've written and we'll talk about it. I'll help you get started. That's the hardest part."

So I did. I sent her one of my stories and she wrote back, full of praise and suggestions.

Johanna was right. Getting started was the hardest part.

Something was still unsettled, through. A memory niggled at the edge of my mind, intruding itself into my new resolve to write every day. Finally, in an attempt to quiet it, I flipped through my folder of Meaningful Sayings, and there it was. The Talmudic quotation:

"When the student is ready the teacher appears."

I made a sign to hang right over the stone that sits on my desk while I write. When I'm stuck I stare at it. I swear that tiger's eye winks back.

16

Coach

I'M SITTING AT MY favorite table in the diner waiting for her to arrive, wondering, *How will I know it's her?* We'd talked on the phone but what she'd told me wasn't much, just that she was starting this new business, she'd be coming from an hour away, and that she'd been living in a yurt. After that, we'd agreed to get together to talk.

As the waitress brought my first cup of coffee, I asked myself, *What do you wear if you live in a yurt these days? I know, I can just see it: long batik skirt, off-white Mexican cotton blouse, sandals with socks because it's late Fall, just turning cold.* But that's if it's 1972. I didn't know about today.

Then standing in front of me, there she was, somehow I knew instantly. Wearing: short black skirt, tight gray turtleneck, black and white herringbone tweed jacket. Coral beads, hair pulled back in the current style. *That's what they're wearing in yurts in 2002?*

She knew it was me, too. Probably the pad of paper I had on the table in front of me gave me away. "Hello," she said, and not waiting for a reply, she slid gracefully into the chair across from me. "You're Jesse, aren't you? I like that name."

Let me explain how we arrived at this moment. I'd been obsessing in the Women's Group, who are, as you know, the people privy to all my concerns—describing how lonely writing is, how after I've written something I can't tell if it's any good or not (maybe it's brilliant?) then I get stuck and have trouble getting myself back on track. *Kvetch, kvetch*. But mostly I've been telling them about how I've been trying to find someone to give me feedback I can use. That I can really use. I'd tried my brothers—one of them kept talking about how I misplaced commas, that I used colons incorrectly—or friends, who just raved about how brave my writing was. So far no one's been the right fit. I've been looking for someone to help me improve the writing itself. Since I've never taken a writing class, I'm plagued by the problems of the self-taught. And since I don't really want to go back to school to get an MFA, it's really that I need a coach.

After our most recent group meeting, I got an email from Maggie, telling me about an announcement she'd just received from a friend of a friend; it was from a Barbara, describing her new consulting business designed to help women develop their writing. Technical writing, poetry, short stories, novels, it didn't matter, Barbara could help. The timing was perfect and, even though it sounded too good to be true, I jumped at the opportunity. Maybe my coach had found me. I emailed Barbara immediately, introducing myself, which is how I came to be waiting at this diner.

Our conversation started smack in the middle; Barbara told me she had gotten an MFA from Iowa, she was a painter and she was a writer. "My writing is sparkling, original, so unique that I've yet to find a publisher who recognizes the true brilliance of my art. I am expert at entering into another person's world and helping bring forth the essence of *their* story without imposing my own style."

Sounds just right, I thought, always wary of being told what to do. I wanted help, but I wanted to retain what I thought of as my own fresh voice.

Barbara went on, describing life in the yurt, which, she explained, was a short-term arrangement. "My goal is to help the yurt owner deal with his energy block to get his creative juices flowing again. I can deal with male energy" she leaned forward, confidentially. "I have my space and he has his." Pausing for a sip of by-now-cool coffee, she added, "We don't have any trouble. I just tell him when he's talking trash."

Fascinating.

But where was I in this conversation? I was interviewing her, it's true, but I hadn't asked a single question (me, the former professional question-asker). *Shouldn't she want to know about my writing, what I'm looking for?* I could try to interject, or I could wait and see what was coming next.

And here it comes.

"I'm more focused now," Barbara said. "When I was younger I was all over the map, I lived in Hawaii and Kenya, as well as the Midwest, Alaska and New Mexico. I guess you could call me a roaming literary artist. When I lived in the Southwest I stayed with Native shamans, they honored me as a visionary. I've been married and divorced, two grown sons. I used to be chasing orgasms, but now I'm done with all that. I've focused my energy on helping other people discover their creative selves. I offer an Interactive Visionary Landscape Forum, a three-day retreat. It only costs $425, but there are scholarships available if that's too much. I believe in taking my work to the people who need it most. I can guarantee that it will energize and revitalize your writing. Do you want to come to the next one? I have a brochure with me."

Uh, let me think it over.

My turn to talk. I tried to slow my spinning head by beginning with the basics: single mother with two kids, two dogs, my partner, Anna. The lesbian part gave Barbara pause for a half-beat and then she cut in, "We all need to develop our other-gendered selves. What are you writing about? I'd love to see what you've got there," she pointed to the red folder I had by now shoved under my writing pad.

Other-gendered selves?

I culled through the stories and gave her two that were the least personal. Barbara grabbed them enthusiastically, got to run, another appointment to get to. "I want to read this" waving the folder, "I'll get back to you within the week. We can discuss my fee then."

I staggered out into the late October day, bright sun, cool air with winter trailing right behind. Minus my two stories.

Deep breath. *What was that?*

Just two days later I received an email from Barbara assuring me that an envelope would be arriving soon with my stories and her comments. "Loved what I read. Got some suggestions. When can we meet? P.S.: Spent more than six hours on your work. Can discuss my fee when we see each other."

The oversized manila envelope arrived, decorated with yin/yang stickers, stuffed with legal-size yellow paper covered in handwritten notes, with comments scribbled between the lines and along the margins in hot, fluorescent pink ink: "You have now told the reader you are examining and sizing-up people—what about embellishing this neurosis—make the writer's edgy nosy guts more obvious." Statement, not question. And: "Do you know you compare the awestruckness of girl. Some people let themselves have visions. The WATER SYMBOL."

Where are the question marks?

Some of this was obviously notes written to herself which I wasn't meant to understand. But in the middle of it all: "Consider showing a bit more emotional tension to add energy to the text." And: "It's like you never go inward enough for me to be able to cry, even though I wanted to." Clanging bell, flashing light: *she's right.*

Then the clincher, a message that afternoon, "I'll be available between 2:00 and 3:00. Call then." *They have phones in yurts these days?* On the phone she was full of praise. "I feel like I'm getting to know you through your stories, but I'd have to know you better to direct this to grow. The best thing would be for me to come over to your house on Sunday night, and then we can get up first thing in the morning, have our coffee—I love French roast, don't you?—go for a walk and get started. I find it works well to be outside and moving when we work."

Thank you, Barbara. But no. What do I owe you for your time?

I got out of it $300 poorer, but at least I didn't have a new roommate.

Alone again. Just me and my writing.

A couple of days later I called Dorothy. She had been sick, so we didn't have regular sessions anymore, but still kept in touch. I told her all about my conversations with Barbara, partly to get it off my chest and partly to make her laugh. Once we were done making jokes about yurts and male energy and being a visionary, she had a suggestion. She gave me the name of someone who taught creative writing at the local college. Maybe she'd be available.

Oh, no. I didn't want to reject Dorothy's idea out of hand, but I could not risk another Barbara. I thanked her with a noncommittal, "I'll think about it."

The suggestion simmered, and after a couple of days I realized I had trusted everything else Dorothy had told me, even when it seemed totally outlandish. Why not this? So I went ahead and wrote the woman, this Miriam, who responded immediately, describing her new business working with writers. (Thankfully, she did not mention the water symbol or letting myself have visions—not yet, anyway—so I felt it was safe to take the next step.) Could we get together to discuss a possible working arrangement? She told me how to recognize her, and we agreed to meet at a restaurant near her office. I drove an hour north, found the designated meeting place, sat down at a table to wait.

Miriam arrived, wearing what everyone wears this time of year in our part of the country: jeans, corduroy work shirt, hiking boots. I knew it was her by the writing pad she was carrying, the way she scanned the people sitting at tables, looking for me. She had short, frizzy black hair. We could have been sisters.

This was different. Miriam started by asking about me, what I was looking for. She explained what she could offer. *Thank God, she has her own place to live.* We agreed to a provisional working arrangement to see if we clicked.

I sent her some stories, she sent me comments, I sent her revisions, she sent me encouragement and more suggestions. She hated my punctuation (*you mean Isaac was right, after all?*). I started to be able to write more often, enjoying it more, learning from her criticism and the endless rewriting. Energized, my writing revitalized, I discovered I could sit at my desk for hours. I had to force myself to stop, go for a walk.

It clears my head to be outside, moving. When I'm walking my thoughts wander and often I discover I'm chewing over a problem that's been troubling me. One day, a month or so after I started working with Miriam, I was taking my usual trek in the country, on a high road that winds past fields where sheep graze. As I strode past the sheep, trying to unravel a problem, it hit me; I was having trouble accepting Miriam's comments. Even though she was sensitive, I'd become bristly. I wanted her to *love* everything I wrote. Now that we'd gotten past the honeymoon stage, deeper into the work, I needed an attitude that would make me more coachable.

"Miriam is your coach," I turned to the sheep. "Listen to what Miriam says!" I admonished them as they chewed their breakfast, unperturbed. One final shout (but first I made them promise they'd never repeat what they heard). They barely lifted their heads as I walked by at a fast clip, proclaiming, "*MIRIAM IS A WRITING G-O-D!*"

The next night while I was luxuriating in the bath, mind drifting as I sank into hot water, the telephone rang, jangling me, and I realized, shaking my head, that I had been having a fantasy about a phone call. From Miriam.

My bath fantasy: I would write something so great she couldn't contain herself, she'd just have to call me up right away. I'd answer: "Oh, Jesse, that's just a fabulous story. It's so good I can't find one thing to criticize. I just *had* to call you."

Well, that didn't happen, exactly. It was a telemarketer asking if I'd like a three-day all-expenses-paid vacation to Disney World. Which I didn't. (We were both disappointed.)

But what it made me realize is that Miriam is in my head. She may not really be The Writing God, but she's offering me help I can use, she's keeping me company and I'm not lonely. Finding a coach has paid off after all.

17

6 Hens and a Robin

Although I'd adjusted my attitude and felt I was making good progress with Miriam, when she suggested I sign up for a writers' conference, I read some criticism. Even though what she said was true—"Writing is lonely, Jesse, as you know. It'll be good to meet people on the same journey"—I still didn't want to go; I just couldn't imagine myself going. Noah and I had been locked in combat. He was home for the summer after his freshman year, bristling with that exquisite blend of condescension and frustration (aged to perfection at eighteen years), his superior knowledge of the world. Taking it out on Mommy.

We snarled, turning away to catch our breath, then strained at invisible leashes, ready to sink teeth into what used to be loving flesh.

I hated leaving. *What will happen while I'm away? What am I getting myself into?* Though it was obvious what I was getting myself out of.

The drive north demanded I shift my furious energy to the road, slick with mid-afternoon rain. Which forced some disengagement, created a tiny opening. I found the campus easily, though I'd come prepared—my bumper sticker NOT ALL WHO WANDER ARE LOST accompanies me wherever I go—just in case I need to look like there's a purpose to my meandering.

I checked in and was directed to a dorm room which seemed unnaturally narrow, crowded with two single beds, two small desks, two bureaus, side-by-side closets, one mirror that only reflects the upper half of your body. *Only my body, thank God, I paid more not to have a roommate.*

Because as soon as I entered that room with the off-green, cinder block walls it's 1967, I'm seventeen, my parents have just deposited me, and I can barely breathe the air is so stale around me.

I left my stuff unpacked, fleeing the nightmare room, to go to my second most hated thing, eating alone in a crowded cafeteria where I don't know anyone. Where I'll have to sidle up to a complete stranger, "Can I join you?" and make polite, meaningless conversation while I struggle to hear, because my hearing aid may be unobtrusive, but it doesn't work well over the clatter of a crowd of hungry people eating bad food.

But wait. Isn't that Miriam waving to me? *She's the one who encouraged me to come, she got me into this.* She gets up to hug me and ushers me over to her table, introducing me. "Welcome, join us." I'm eating at the faculty table.

I can hear Miriam and the man on my other side, both of them have big voices. The food's not half bad. After dinner and the opening reception we'll meet our workshop leader and fellow writers.

Settling into the small reading room off the library filled with stuffed armchairs, we begin with a brief go-around, typical introductions: *tell us a little about yourself, and what you hope to get out of the conference.* We are six women, who look to be youngish to oldish, with me at fifty-four in the older half. The sole male is the leader—*of course*, I complain to myself, *isn't that typical?* I'm first after Robin, our leader, and while I intended to talk about my writer-self, I hear my own voice declaring, "I live in Middlesex, Vermont, I'm a lesbian with two kids, people always wonder how I got the kids, so here goes . . . I had Noah and Sophie by artificial insemination, my then-partner and I started a program in Boston for lesbians who wanted to have children, it was a long time ago before many gay women where having kids, the *gayby* boom, you know . . ." *Whoa, slow down there, who said you had to say all that?*

Thank God, I finally shut up and the woman on my left starts speaking into the stunned silence.

One evening down. Six days to go.

Next morning early, I'm first—again—to be "workshopped." *I didn't know it could be a verb,* but anyway, I'm to sit there and listen to comments without responding. I'm good at listening. I cross my legs, open my notebook, pick up my lavender pen, bought especially for this conference, and try to lower my defenses. Even though I desperately want them to love what I've written, just like I've wanted Miriam to be speechless, in awe.

But, no, they have plenty to say—most of which rings true—putting into words just what I've been worried about in the stories they're critiquing. They tell me just what's wrong. And make suggestions about how to fix it.

My hour is up, time for just one final comment: "I want the mother to be a knitter. Then the narrator can be the dropped stitch. It's a no-brainer."

What? what? Jesse can't knit. Who should? The mother should knit? A no-brainer?

Oh, my God, you're right. I get it.

I have to fight to stay in my chair, calmly writing *no brainer, mother knits* in lavender ink, while everything shifts and slides into place inside my story.

The next morning it's someone else's turn. We've all read her twenty-five pages and leap in, walking the tightrope, balancing the gentle and the critical. And so the mornings go, one, two, three. An unspoken decision has been made to resist assigned seats, so we end up sitting next to a new person every day. Except for Robin who chose a chair the first evening and continues to occupy it. We each have our own trajectory, but we are always in relation to Robin.

Robin, who listens, comments, tells his own stories. Without condescending, without flaunting his experience, even though he really *is* a published author and a writing professor. Thereby calling into question all my assumptions about men-in-charge, dominating in groups of women.

We listen carefully when he talks, but no more closely than when the youngest member tells her story. She was poisoned as a teenager, nearly died before an accurate diagnosis was made and proper treatment given. Robin tells us that no one should be the hero of their own memoir—and maybe not—but in that room for that week, everyone was a hero in my eyes.

Thank you, Miriam, for making me come. Being here on campus, in the dorm room where I was seventeen again, forced me to release my fingers from around Noah's throat. Being in the room with the other fledgling writers and Robin, a teacher who refused to be a hero, gave me space to catch my breath, to be myself distinct and separate from my Mommy-self.

I arrived not knowing why I'd come, afraid I'd get lost, found something I needed, and wanted to leave with a joke.

Something about being birds of a feather—all us hens, you see—for that week. Six hens and a robin.

18

Getting the Mail

So I'd retired but somehow not working was more work than I'd imagined. Because I hadn't yet figured out what to do with all the time on my hands, how to make a schedule for myself. My morning routine looked like this: up at 6:30, encourage showers, help make lunches and see the kids off to the school bus. By 7:30 I'd be sitting at my desk with my first cup of coffee, staring at the blank computer screen, intimidated and blank myself. With any luck I would start to write. I'd last about an hour or, if it was a good day and I felt brave and determined, an hour and a half. Then I'd start looking around, trying to find something meaningful-but-not-too-demanding to do until 11:00 when I could go get the mail. Which was the high point of my morning, at least for the fifteen minutes it took me to walk to the end of the driveway and sort through the junk, looking for something relatively interesting while I strolled back to the house. This almost always proved a disappointment, since I rarely found anything that merited a second look. But at least it wasn't too taxing.

One morning recently, I went on my mail run and what I found was beyond relatively interesting; it tilted my world. Mixed in with everything else, I spotted a letter from Aunt Judith which promised to be more interesting than junk (but required a bit more effort than I appreciate in the morning). I've endured a lifetime of Aunt Judith's illegible handwriting. She's a true Silverman, of the type my mother deplored: her envelopes arrive stuffed-to-overflowing with articles on some esoteric subject from *The New York Times* or *The Nation* with scrawly notes up and down the margins that I'm sure add depth and insight, but what good does it do me if I can't decipher a word? Later Aunt Judith will call to ask what I think of the article and her commentary, and I'll have to make up something halfway intelligent to say.

Luckily, this time the letter was typed. The paper was yellowed, the print faded. When I unfolded the pages gently along well-worn creases, I was afraid it would fall to pieces in my hands. *What's this? And how old is it?*

In Case of death only, please send this to:

> Mrs. Solomon L. Silverman
> 2257 Indianola Ave., Columbus, Ohio, USA

Do *not* send in case of injury.

Thanks, comrade.
Benjamin Silverman

Dear Mother and Father:

I suppose that by the time you receive this, I will have been dead several weeks. Of course, war is a confused thing, and I have seen enough certified corpses walking around to make me a little skeptical, but if you receive this and an official announcement too, count it as definite.

This is the last day of relief. We are going up to some front tomorrow to clear out the Fascists. I do not doubt that we will be successful in repatriating the boys across the street, but it will be at considerable cost, and as the Lincoln Battalion is good it should be in the middle of it.

I still stick by my original conviction that I will be alive long after a whole lot of dictators have died of lead poisoning or hardened arteries; but I have been wrong on other matters before. Hence I decided to write this letter.

Certainly I am not enthusiastic about dying. I have gotten a good bit of fun out of my first twenty years despite the fact that, except for the last six months, they were pretty useless. I suppose I would have enjoyed my next twenty just as much. I wanted to write this letter, however, to make clear that there is absolutely nothing to regret.

If I were alive again I think I would join in the battle again at this crucial place. There was an extremely important job to do over here and I was one of the men who decided to do it. That a good many of us were killed while doing it is unfortunate, and the fact that I was killed is still more unfortunate from our standpoints. However, this has no relevance to the necessity of doing the job. The difference between world Fascism and world socialism is far too great to permit our safeties to be a factor for consideration.

Next I want to beg both of you not to see this out of context. World change is a stern master. It has killed and will kill millions of boys as dear to somebody as I am to you. The Fascists want war, and bitter war we will give them.

You are more fortunate than many of the parents, for you still have two children with extremely bright futures. You have your extremely valuable work. I am less able to evaluate Father's work, though I realize its great worth; but in my field, that of an author, I can say I think Mother should become one of the most valuable authors of the generation. And you still have the emancipation of America to be achieved.

I think my ideas on immortality agree largely with yours. I once wrote a lousy poem "If there is darkness beyond I shall sleep, if light I shall wake." So if I meet you folks again all to the good—if not, we've had quite a bit of pleasure in each other's company while it lasted.

As for my friends, give them my love if you run across them. Tell them I said there's only one thing to remember—that there's one comrade less to do the job of soldier of discontent. They'll all have to do some work to make up for my getting perforated. See if that will get a few of these mugwumps into action.

This has been a clumsy letter. I just wanted to say that I love you both a great deal, and so forth. Also that it isn't such a serious thing.

Love and revolutionary greetings.
Joy to the world.
Benjamin

And on the very bottom of the page in Judith's scrawl: "August or September 1937."

I stood, riveted. I'd just met one of the most important people in my life, the man who'd affected us all though he was hardly more than a boy when he died. Here was the person who had something to do with who we all were. Here was the person who had everything to do with who my father was. My father, just fifteen when his hero, Benjamin, died in Spain fighting fascism. Standing there in the driveway halfway up the steep hill to my house, I stood staring through a window at a view sixty-five years old.

Having met his big brother, I caught a glimpse of the boy my father had been, the losses he'd absorbed, the man he would become. How principles became his religion. What kind of father he was. What he couldn't give.

My life was new, altered forever, as I marched back to the house, holding Benjamin's letter like a treasure. The problems that had plagued me—how to spend my time, what to write—gone. Vanquished. First Vincent, and now this. The message was unmistakable, echoing across the years. The dead boy had spoken: care about the world, be brave and passionate, find a cause and join up.

Too Big

19

Too Big

*E*VERY MORNING EARLY, I drove Sophie to school, hurrying home to Anna in bed, anticipating the heat of our bodies together. This was what I'd yearned for my whole life—what I didn't know I was missing—this uninhibited moaning and howling with delight, which made the outside world disappear.

I was almost home when I saw a car in front of me with a license plate, one of those vanity plates you can buy. It said: TOO BIG.

Which took my breath away, I had to pull over onto the shoulder to talk to myself: *Breathe, Jesse, breathe.*

When I finally breathed myself back home, all desire and thoughts of Anna had been banished. I was empty.

Seeing that emptiness, Anna placed her hand on my back, a quiet touch in the place I hold all my deepest feelings—the things you can't say out loud to anyone.

"Jesse, what's wrong?"

How can I tell her?

When Thomas molested Sophie she still sucked her thumb, making her seem younger than the five years she was so proud of.

There was so much to take care of right after she told, so many things that demanded my immediate attention: therapy appointments for her, facing the crippling guilt that I'd allowed this to happen.

Anna knew that Sophie had been molested, but not the details. This daughter she had grown to love—how could I tell my lover what had really happened to her?

It was impossible to explain TOO BIG. How could I risk the tidal wave of her rage that threatened to sweep us both away? *I'm not strong enough to save us both.*

Sophie, somehow, found words. She had told me. In bits and pieces.

That first morning: "Thomas tried to put his penis in my vagina. He made grunting noises, like, like"—always the animal-lover she searched for the right description—"like a pig. He made me promise not to tell you."

That was all she said the first time. Which was enough to change our lives forever. Even the constant reassurance: "You did the right thing telling me, you didn't do anything wrong, Sophie, it wasn't your fault" over and over again, that litany of reassurance, the changes were enough to shut her up.

Then slowly—usually at night when I put her to bed, after reading her a story, then singing a song, then lying down with her because now she was scared of the dark—she told more.

"Mommy, why did he do that to me? All I did was ask where babies came from . . ."

Another night: "Was it my fault because I asked that question?"

And then: "I told him to stop. I told him it hurt. That it was too big."

The night I heard that, lying beside her in bed, that was the night I re-froze, exactly in the place of deepest breath. And stayed that way for years, so long that the pain became part of me. So long that the freeze felt normal.

Until Anna came, Anna who brought enough fire for two and I started to thaw. But thawing hurt. Disarmed, no longer frozen, even a license plate with TOO BIG could penetrate my soft shell.

Only Sophie told the truth:

"Mommy, when you talk about that time, you always say that Thomas molested me. But Mommy, you're wrong. I was raped."

20

Binky

That day in September when terrorists crashed planes into buildings, as people leapt from certain death to certain death, and the television ensured we saw it all in living color, that night eleven-year-old Sophie took to sleeping with me again. Her child's sense of invincibility re-shattered, after all our effort to put the pieces of her life back together. It had taken her a long time to stop sucking her thumb, to get used to staying in her own bed, but by ten, she'd managed it. Now here she was in my room, standing beside the bed, sniffling, eyes downcast. I patted the place beside me and she crawled in, snuggling under the covers.

"You know," she began, loving to talk and explain herself, "I think *you're* my security blanket. I don't really feel safe without you."

"Well, this is a very hard time," I agreed. "Everyone's feeling worried and insecure. You can stay as long as you need to," I said, hoping it wouldn't be all that long.

"I think you're my binky," she went on, patting my hand. "Binky, binky." Pleased with the new nickname, she dropped into sleep.

Binky.

Feeling afraid and sad and insecure isn't new—these tentacles reach back to when she was little, way before giant buildings crashed to the ground and she watched it all on TV.

As you know, just after her fifth birthday she was raped by Thomas, Brenda's twelve-year-old son. We'd been struggling to create a family for a couple of years, but even before the unimaginable happened, we'd been in trouble. That lovely July evening when it happened, Brenda and I had gone out alone on a rare date in a relationship whose main focus had shifted to Thomas and his problems. Thomas's father had abandoned him when he was five and had just now reappeared—jumping into our lives like a jack-in-the-box—without warning. Brenda was furious at him (*for disappearing, for reappearing, for leaving her with a "problem child"?*) she could barely snarl his name. There had been precious little room for an *us* to develop, so this date was a special event. We had left Sophie and Thomas at home with a babysitter. Noah wasn't home, he spent most weekends with Ruth.

Both kids were asleep in their rooms when we got back. I drove the sitter home and then climbed into bed with Brenda, exhausted, but happy to curl up to her sleepy warmth, pleased we'd had time together even though we hardly knew what to say to each other any more. *Maybe things will get better now that we've made a start.*

I woke up the next morning, startled by the sense of eyes on me. Sophie leaning over me, "Mommy, I want be with you," she said, not climbing in, like she usually did. Still half-asleep, I rolled out of bed and followed her into the TV room to snuggle on the couch. I was trying to hold on to some last vestiges of sleep, when she pulled away and sat up.

"Mommy, last night Thomas tried to put his penis in my vagina."

What?

"What?"

"I asked him where babies came from and he said he'd show me. He made me promise not to tell anyone."

What is she saying?
Is it possible she could make this up?
No, impossible. She'd never in a million years be able to make up something so explicit.

Holding Sophie's hand tight, I walked her into the bedroom and shook Brenda awake, even though it was before six, and she hated early mornings. There was hell to pay if anyone woke her on weekends.

Sophie perched on the edge of the bed while Brenda struggled to open her eyes, dazed and sour. *There better be a good reason for this*, the look on her face said to me. I put my arm around Sophie. "Sweetie, can you tell Brenda what you just told me?" She did, sounding even younger than her five-year-old self. Instantly awake, Brenda tore out of bed, flying into Thomas's room.

That was the last we saw of her for hours. We could hear Thomas wailing and Brenda bellowing, "You what?" Sobbing. Screams. His, hers? Both of them intermingling? Silence as terrifying as the screams. Sophie and I sat on the bed, holding hands, waiting. Somehow, I was still hoping—praying really—that Sophie had misunderstood what had happened.

But could she have misunderstood penis and vagina?

When Brenda finally did come out of Thomas's room, it was to tell me she was taking him out of the house, away from me.

Away from me?

"You're so angry you might hurt him. I'm going to take him to see his father, so we can talk to him together. You have to stay in the bedroom with Sophie so I could leave the house without Thomas having to see you."

Brenda was protecting Thomas from me?

I sat there immobilized, my five-year-old now sucking her thumb, leaning into me. "I made Be-Be mad at me," she whimpered, "and Thomas won't like me anymore because I told."

Words caught and died, extinguished. I was left cuddling Sophie as Brenda and her son made their furtive, silent exit.

We were divided into teams now, the fault line underlying our relationship—the fact of us never having been a family—revealed in stark relief.

Alone in the suddenly empty house, we retreated into routine, Sophie sucking her thumb, while I stumbled through the ritual of morning coffee. Then, not knowing how to face an impossibly changed world, I did the most familiar thing: I called the women in my group. Not one of them was home. I left messages with a plea for someone to call me.

Our home had become toxic. "Hey, Sophie, want to go out to breakfast?"

Driving back to check for messages, I missed a curve and swerved off the road. Sophie stared at me as we sat in the car, unhurt, trembling, as I tried to slow my ragged breaths.

The rest of what happened that day is a blur, but I remember the night because it turned into a nightmare. We followed Sophie's usual bedtime routine. I read her a story, got her a glass of water, sang her a song. Then, "Mommy, will you lie down with me?"

"Of course." And fell asleep in her bed curled beside her.

Later, Brenda walked past the bedroom. Filling the doorway, she hissed, "What are you doing in there?"

"I'm lying down with Sophie," I whispered. "She's upset and she asked me to sleep with her."

"You can't do that. You're making her more upset, because you're so upset. You're making it worse by catering to her."

I hadn't been doing anything wrong of course, but now I did. Something so wrong it tore a hole in the fabric of my definition of myself as a good mother.

I left my sleeping daughter. I went upstairs to lie beside Brenda, stiff, afraid of making her any madder than she already was. Afraid she would leave. Afraid to be alone.

As it turned out—of course—she found a way to blame me and, in a rage, moved out of the house where we had pretended to be a family. And I *was* alone, living with the reality that I'd sacrificed a precious moment with my own child to try to keep a lover;

a lover who couldn't be kept. I let misplaced desire and insecurity blind me.

A bitter lesson. But once I woke up to it, I made myself a solemn promise: any time either of the kids feels scared or insecure, about *anything*, there are no excuses. None. I vowed that I will stay where I belong for as long as they need me.

There are worse names your eleven-year-old can call you than Binky. If Sophie needs me, I'll be Binky, even if it lasts a lifetime.

Telling

21

The Letter

*E*ven though we like to believe that our lives are linear—starting here and ending there, with a beginning, middle, and an end—I've come to believe that the whole affair is more like a spiral. We pass one point, "deal with an issue," face it, and put it to rest. But, damn, there you are five or ten or twenty-five years later, and there's the same goddamn "issue." Waiting for you.

I've already told you some about my therapy with Dorothy, the Guide who used astrology to illustrate her points. I've described her approach, including endless journaling and the deep breathing technique where I met Petra for the first time. This was part of the package of the untraditional—some might say kooky—model she used which she called "The Healing Path." She didn't take credit, though; she claimed it had been channeled through her, but I have a hunch it sprang from the depths of her own suffering. But regardless of its source, it became a powerful tool for those of us craving "healing" and "self-actualization," concepts that had great stature in those days of "the worried well"—a category I *guess* I was almost well enough to fit into.

"The Path"—those of us in the inner circle used this shorthand—required that you choose someone who you had unfinished business with. Your task was to understand how you had played out your own issues against the backdrop of the relationship. Then came the work of integrating these insights into a new sense of yourself. There were twelve Steps. I envisioned these as stadium steps, and being in good shape, I imagined I could just dash up them, and be at the top in no time.

And though there weren't really concrete steps, there was a distinct final product. A letter. There was something appealing about this, it's very concreteness made it feel substantial, real. Every therapy I'd been in before—and the therapy I'd practiced as a clinician—had a somewhat mysterious and ambiguous end, which often became a point of conflict. How would you know when therapy was over? No clear-cut ending. No final product.

The structure of The Path was clear-cut, too. Those twelve Steps were associated with the signs of the zodiac, a connection I never did grasp, though it was explained to me every time I complained that I couldn't see where we were headed. (Dorothy has got to be one of the most patient women in the world. Can you imagine me as a client? A therapist myself, I knew the lingo and all the tricks for intellectualizing, avoiding, projecting.)

But even while I complained and intellectualized and projected, I did what Dorothy asked me to do. I wrote the required journal. Step Two is where you explore, in fact, sink into, and indulge, your emotions. I'd gotten through Step One, the Commitment Statement, so efficiently I just knew I was a star. *Just like I thought!* I would sprint down the Path to a glorious finish, faster than anyone before me.

So you can imagine how stunned and demoralized I was that it took me two years to complete Step Two. Two whole years. You couldn't step on until Dorothy said you were ready. That's a lot of sinking into your emotions, that's a lot of ventilating on paper. That's almost two hundred pages of white-hot rage.

Finally, Dorothy announced I was ready to move on, I could start writing drafts of the letter. *Thank God, finally.* I was thrilled, until I realized what starting the letter translated into in Path lingo. Emphasize *starting*, emphasize *draft*. Years of drafts lay ahead of me.

The letter was addressed to the person you were "healing" with. I'd chosen Brenda, because our relationship was the most recent disaster in my life. We ended horribly, which was fitting because our final years together had been horrible.

The first Steps were all about *feeling* what had gone on between us. I had done my share of blaming her, seeing myself victimized by her win-at-all-cost approach to disagreements, which turned them into battles, her troubled relationship with Thomas which left no time for intimacy, her volcanic anger. The blaming part came easily.

What came after was harder: recognizing and taking responsibility for my contribution to our troubles. That's where resistance intervened, becoming a palpable presence, and I tripped on my dash to early completion. I still wanted to blame Brenda. It felt accurate, familiar, and true to see her as the Bully and me as the Cowering Innocent.

But as I wrote my way through version-after-endless-version of a letter toward the final Letter, what became obvious were the ways I *had* played my part. Even with my pal *resistance*, chattering at my side, I couldn't avoid seeing it. We had each taken our turn as wounded and wounder.

The first drafts weren't all that difficult to write when I was in blame-mode. I could describe in exquisite detail all the terrible things Brenda did to me. Writing was cathartic, satisfying. What got hard was following Dorothy's instructions to clear away all the critical, cutting barbs, what she called "underbrush."

"Get rid of the snipers, Jesse," she intoned. That wasn't so easy. When I presented her with a bare-bones, pared-down version, no underbrush at all, snipers banished, the next assignment was to *expand* on what I was telling Brenda—"Deepen the sharing, fully express the experience."

And when I had completed that, tell her what I had learned from the relationship. What I was grateful for.

Oh, great. Sure: Thank you for screaming at me, thank you for giving me the silent treatment for days on end, thanks so much for ignoring me sexually.

I tried that on Dorothy.

Guess not. She laughed sympathetically, "Yes, it is painful. Now you need to get back to the letter. No sarcasm, no sniping allowed."

What the hell did that leave me with?

Then I went back to my silent complaining, overwhelmed by the daunting prospect of having to face my own part in the mess. That went on, until finally, I calculated how much money I'd wasted, wrestling with resistance or mired by inertia. That's when I got sick of my internal cringing, took my own hand, and truly stepped onto the Healing Path. I settled in for the long haul, and wrote another version of the letter.

> *Dear Brenda,*
>
> *I remember the last thing I said when you were moving out of the Brigham Road house: "I have so much to be grateful for." Seems like a strange thing to say at a time like that and since then I've often wondered what I meant.*
>
> *Since we split up I've been trying to untangle and understand what happened in our relationship. This has been very painful but also emotionally clarifying. In many ways our relationship, difficult though it was, has been a vehicle for me to unravel parts of myself that I never fully understood before. And I'm grateful for that.*
>
> *Several months after we'd been separated, following a particularly nasty fight, you offered me the opportunity to get together and, in your words, "scream at me all you want." I declined then, but now I'd like you to listen to what I've come to see about our time together.*
>
> *Examining our relationship has helped me recognize the ways we are alike, as well as the ways we're different. In the past I wanted to blame you for all the bad things that happened and for how hurt I felt. Now I realize that I contributed to my own pain, and I can see the ways I must have hurt you.*
>
> *Looking back I realize that when we were together I was almost always afraid: afraid of making you angry, afraid that you would leave me, afraid that I was staying in a situation that was bad for my kids, and—most damaging—afraid I was a bad mother for not being able to leave. I became anx-*

ious, worried and depressed. I came to feel that you didn't really like me very much, let alone love me, so I kept trying to do things I thought you'd like and behave in ways I thought you'd approve of. This backfired of course, as it always does, and I grew to hate the person I was becoming.

I can see now that the fact that I couldn't find a way to love Thomas must have hurt you deeply because, of course, he is your son and you love him. This must have been unbearable, and I'm sorry for that.

It seemed like it was easier for you to focus on the fact that Thomas and I didn't get along than to acknowledge his emotional problems. I felt like you blamed me for his troubles. I became the scapegoat. You acted like I'd caused his problems, but the reality is that I'd inherited most of them. So our relationship as a "family" was a mess even before the sexual incident that blew the lid off.

It was impossible then, and it feels almost impossible now, to say clearly what Thomas did to Sophie. When I used the word "molested," you got furious and insisted it was "sex play." So let's dispense with terms or euphemisms and state straight out what happened. Sophie told us, unembellished, "Thomas tried to put his penis in my vagina." That's it. Call it what you like, those are the facts.

I can see now that you were in an emotionally impossible situation because you loved both kids. But since Sophie was our shared child I expected you'd be there for her, too. I can see that this was naive. You abandoned her because your energy was devoted entirely to figuring out how to help Thomas. And then when you told Thomas I was angry because I'd been molested as a child, I felt angry and betrayed. That was just dead wrong. Your explanation was just a way of explaining away my reaction. I reacted the way any mother would have, the way you yourself would have, if Thomas hadn't been your son.

There's so much that's happened since then that you don't know about. Sophie says there are pictures in her mind that get in the way of being able to concentrate in school. She needs to leave her classroom to go talk to the school nurse when these pictures come. She drew a circle with a penis with a red line through it. She's in therapy. Most of the time *she seems fine on the surface, but I can't ever tell when she'll blurt out, "I loved him like a brother. Why did Thomas do that to me? Was it my fault?" So you see I can't "just get over it" as you suggested, because Sophie's not "over it."*

But even before this happened, we were in trouble. I knew you'd withdrawn from me, both sexually and emotionally. I felt dismissed when we did try to talk, so eventually I just shut up and silenced myself. This may have kept the peace for a while, but it killed me inside. What I've come to realize is that what you told me about myself is true: my anger was buried and it could "leak out" onto you. Our house was a toxic waste site. We both contributed to the contamination.

I want to acknowledge the baggage I brought with me that contributed to the death of our relationship. I had certain beliefs about myself: that I was "too intense," that if anyone discovered my flaws they would stop loving me, that some person or force outside myself had the power to comfort or abandon me. I can see now that you became that person in my unconscious script. Hardly the stuff of an equal relationship between peers. We were doomed from the start.

There's one thing we do agree about, that the Universe offers us the lessons we need to learn. Our relationship, though wholly imperfect, taught me this:

1. *Do not assume you can change someone's basic personality and temperament. Love them as they are or don't get involved with them.*
2. *Never settle for less than you deserve, to be loved fully with all your human flaws and frailties.*
3. *Don't worry about being alone. It is far better than being in a relationship where you feel invisible or victimized.*
4. *Do not accept being silenced, by another person or by your own internal critic.*
5. *Demand open communication and honesty from your loved one and from yourself. Accept nothing less.*
6. *Make time to enjoy all your passions, including sexual pleasures. Don't ever give this up. It is one of life's gifts.*
7. *Find your own special voice and use it.*

That being said, what I'm grateful to you for is the opportunity to learn these lessons.

I thought the letter was terrific, snipers banished, underbrush cleared away. Dorothy didn't agree, she thought there was still more work to be done, "You're 80% of the way there."

I just couldn't keep on with the revisions, though. I didn't have the energy or, frankly, the desire to work on that last 20%. Dorothy respected my decision and suggested that it was time to take a break. Maybe I'd come back to the letter, maybe I wouldn't. She let me go.

I didn't intend to send the letter, but not because it wasn't complete. I realized that now I didn't need to say these things to Brenda, I didn't need anything from her any more. I'd figured out what I needed to by doing my own work, and had integrated what I learned. Maybe not perfect healing, but good enough.

That would have been the end of it. I would have walked away complete enough, except that the planets lined up or some other inexplicable New Age phenomenon occurred that eroded my previous resolve. Something unnameable breathed in my ear, and I mailed the letter.

If Brenda responded—and I wasn't at all sure she would—I knew exactly what she'd say. I could already hear her "go fuck yourself" snarl, that killer combination of words and tone.

So I had my armor ready whenever I picked through the mail, or answered the phone.

No letter. *See, I knew she wouldn't even pay me the courtesy of answering. Good thing I didn't need that. I did it for myself.*

So when I answered the phone a week later I'd dropped my guard, and by the time I recognized Brenda's voice, it was too late to scramble back into my armor.

"I'm in awe of the work you must have done to be able to write that letter," she said.

So who was the real Brenda and who the imagined?

I'd written two hundred pages in exquisite detail describing the woman who would have respond with that dismissive, ugly "fuck you." I'd known her intimately. Hadn't I?

Is it possible she wasn't really a Nazi? How much did I misunderstand, see through the lens of my own misery? How much of our story am I going to have to revise?

In the four years I'd been slogging along the Healing Path, maybe Brenda had been completing and integrating in her own way, I don't know. I just know that her opening "I'm in awe" gave us a chance, opened a dialogue that I never, in a million years, would have believed possible. Then having chanced the impossible—talked civilly, listened respectfully—we each turned away, breathed deeply—*thank God, that's over*—and scrambled back to our separate paths.

22

The Hero

BEN AND I WERE finally talking. "Did Mom and Dad drink when we were kids?" You'd think I'd know something important like this, but I didn't, and I knew that Ben probably would. He remembered everything. I needed help filling in the blanks. "I know that Ginger and Betty's parents were heavy drinkers." No one used the word *alcoholic* then, and it seemed disrespectful, even more than thirty years later, to introduce it now.

"Well," Ben said, "they drank every afternoon after the men got home from the University. They always said it was 'so goddamn hot' they deserved a drink. Bob and Jean would come over and they'd all sit on the patio on those rattan chairs—you remember those?—and drink gin and tonics. They'd curse the heat, they'd talk politics, commiserating with each other about being Yankees in Louisiana which they said was the most redneck state in the redneck Deep South. As the drinks went down, they'd congratulate each other on being an island of civility surrounded as they were by bigots and racists. Let's just say they didn't have much of an idea where we all were, or what we were up to. When we started going on adventures, I was eight, the oldest, so I took charge of the gang of us. You were four, then Jon, Ginger and Betty, who we called BB for Betty-Baby, you must remember that. She was just three, and we would've treated her like the baby she was, except we all admired her because she was the best at catching snakes.

Usually when we got home, it'd be dark and no one was in any shape to fix us supper, so I made us all scrambled eggs. You liked them with onions."

You see what I mean about him remembering the details?

Ben was telling me the story of our growing up together in the 1950s in New Orleans, Louisiana, that place where the Civil War hadn't yet been lost, where heat had substance. Humidity drenched us, history hung heavy along with Spanish moss, Jim Crow, and drinking. I never thought much about my parents those days, which is why I was asking Ben all these questions. Because my world was my brothers, running through fields, fishing in the swamps that had more crawfish and snakes than fish, riding bareback on the neighbors' wild horses. Those were just a few of the things we did that my parents never knew about. That's what I remember, because that's what was important, but you can see Ben remembered other things, too.

When Ben got back to his house after our conversation, he wrote me a story, just like he promised. "Louisiana Days" described our wild time growing up in the bayous.

He wrote it for a reason.

Years before, when he was seventeen and I'd just turned thirteen, we'd played a secret game, called "Tickle Monster," and it started out as just that, tickling, but it turned into something else. I would be laughing hysterically, squealing, "Stop, Stop!" Sometimes he would, but sometimes he wouldn't. He'd touch me, then, in a different way, while I lay, frozen, speechless. Until I couldn't anymore, and I finally told on us.

Here's that problem with terminology again: what do you call what happened between us? Was it innocent sex play, or molestation, or sexual abuse? Whatever it's called, after that first telling, I dedicated a lifetime of energy to not telling again.

In a family so conventional, so focused on doing-the-right-thing, even now it's hard to understand how this could happen. What part did the fact that we all worshiped Ben—that he was our undisputed hero—play? When I was twelve we had left the embattled South for upstate New York, and that year Ben became the unrivaled love of my life. I liked some boys in my seventh grade class, and had even gone on a date with the class clown, but nothing could compete with my big brother spending time with me. He was seventeen, shy and handsome. Smart and brave, too.

One wintry day when we were out climbing in the gorges—something our mother had strictly forbidden—I got stuck on a ledge. The shale was crumbly and slippery, covered with icy mist from the waterfall so far below that it was out of sight. I'd gotten halfway across before paralyzing fear grabbed me and I couldn't move forward along the narrow outcropping, and there wasn't room for me to turn around and go back. Sensing my panic from the other side, Ben crept toward me, his hand extended, talking me along the rock path to safety. I never forgot that. He was my big brother, and he protected me.

So when the wrestling started it was just another fun thing we did together. We'd start off kidding around on my bed, rolling over and over until finally he'd pin me. Then he'd tickle, but as it got more rambunctious, I squealed for him to stop. That moment right before he quit felt like forever, suspended in time. He would roll away, sitting on the side of the bed. Then he would walk out of my room, shutting his bedroom door quietly behind him, to do homework or whatever else seventeen-year-old boys do. Off into his own world.

Other nights he'd offer to give me a backrub and I would luxuriate in the attention, sometimes he'd stop abruptly, and ask me to give him one. Those times he would compliment me, telling me how good I was with my hands. When I was alone I'd secretly hold out my hands to admire them. More than anything, I wanted to please him, I wanted to do what he wanted. I wanted him to think I was grown-up. Cool.

When the touching started I didn't know what to think. The game was fun until the scary part when he slid his hands under my pajama top, cupping my new breasts. I'd go still, hardly breathing, waiting for him to pull away and leave.

We never said anything to each other after these adventures. We didn't make plans. We'd just end up in my room again. After the first couple of nights, his hands moved down from my breasts to my tummy, then they inched under the elastic waist of my pj bottoms. I stopped him before he got all the way there.

Ben's silent withdrawal left me feeling like I wasn't grown-up and cool at all. I felt sick, fighting constant nausea. I didn't want to lose Ben, but I somehow I knew that it was up to me to stop our game. *But maybe not, maybe this is what big kids do? Maybe this is the same as the other things Mom told us not to do, that we did anyway. But it's even scarier than when I got stuck on the icy ledge. I don't know; I just feel like I'm going to throw up.*

I hated to disappoint Ben. *Please, please don't let him get mad at me.* But I was scared that our mother would find out and that *she'd* get mad. I didn't know who I was most afraid of making mad.

After I told Ben I wasn't playing anymore, he didn't ask why, he just nodded, staring past me, and stopped coming to my room. Now that there wasn't anything to be upset about, I should have felt better, but the sick feeling didn't go away. Ben had asked me not to tell anyone; this was a special secret just between us.

I promised him. I can't tell. He'll never talk to me again.

I tried my hardest, but I couldn't do it, I finally had to tell *someone*, and the someone was our mother.

I hoped that once I got up my courage to start I'd be able to tell her. Because we were a talkative family, every one knew that. Discussions at our dinner table were loud and raucous, ranging from politics, popular music, who was dating who. Everyone had an opinion, and intent on being heard, shouted over whoever had the floor. Nothing was off-limits, or so it seemed. Our mother was the center, she kept us all going. She listened, she cajoled, she gave advice, she sympathized.

When I told her, she wasn't mad. She hardly said a word. I didn't have a clue what she was feeling, and no way to find out.

When we talked about it years later she told me that she'd let me sleep with her in her big bed that night. I don't remember that. What I do remember is that Ben's bedroom got moved downstairs away from the rest of us kids, down with the grown-ups. He never said anything to me about it.

My mother didn't talk to me about it, she told me later, because she didn't know *what* to say. She loved both of us, I know that. I'm left trying to imagine the rest: her horror coupled with disbelief, anger, and searing pain that tore her.

How could he do this to me, my perfect Ben? How am I supposed to go on acting like everything's fine, when all I feel is a gaping wound, my pride as the mother of wonderful, well-behaved children shattered?

Maybe if I don't say a word, no one will know my secret—that I've failed as a mother.

I thought I'd taught him right from wrong. How could I have known I needed to teach him that*? Somehow I failed to protect my sweet Jesse.*

But how the hell would I know I had to protect her from her brother. Now both kids are a mess—not talking about it, but I know—I can feel it.

Goddamn it to hell! How could they put me in this impossible position? How could they do this to me?

Suppers were quieter. Sometimes the tension got to be too much and the younger kids would blurt out, "What's wrong? Are you mad at us?" My mother would just shake her head, and disappear into the kitchen. Ben gulped his food, bolted from the house to go out with his friends. My father, silent as usual, concentrated on the pad of paper beside his plate, where he jotted math equations. Out from under the presiding eye of my mother, the younger boys—Isaac was now old enough to sit in a chair and squirm—enjoyed the freedom of kicks under the table and the occasional tossed carrot. I tried to keep them in line so our mother wouldn't get upset, but they ignored my dire warnings about what would happen if they didn't shut up.

No one had to tell me to be quiet.

Then, without explanation, dinners went back to normal. My mother presided again. The boys stopped kicking. Nothing was wrong.

Silence was supposed to make the problem disappear, and it worked for a while. But eventually this premature burial fed the monster until it grew into an obese bully, demanding attention and exacting a price. Silence was both the price and the punishment.

For all of us. What was unspeakable began to putrify and stink, but never fully rotted away. It became a secret that had to be guarded, at all costs. When you're guarding something that putrid, you get careful—very careful—that nothing leaks out. I grew into a secret-keeper. But what I'd thought was securely buried seeped into everything, polluting, spoiling.

But in a perverse, nameless way, keeping the secret also made me feel *special*, I had new status: protector of my brother and mother. I kept them safe. I accepted permanent guard duty over the monster. But as hard as I tried, I was still a kid, and I failed at my assignment. Instead of staying dead where it was buried like it was supposed to, it grew bigger and bigger, invisible, beneath an ordinary, placid surface.

Years of therapy helped me prepare myself to confront my mother. I developed a script, I acquired armor. I had questions for her. I wanted to be careful to ask just my questions, to try to keep the monster under control, even though sometimes I couldn't tell where I left off and the monster began.

I started with my mother, rather than Ben. I knew she loved me, and trusted that she would still, even after I finished telling her how much her silence had wounded me. I told her everything about how this not-telling had permeated my life, that it had grown toxic, seeping into everything I touched. Once I started there was no turning back: "Mom, what the hell were you thinking? How in God's name did you decide to handle it that way?" My mother listened while I vomited monster-parts all over her.

That was just my opening line. I went on, as you can imagine.

When I had emptied myself, and paused for breath, she explained whose advice she had followed.

"I was just so upset and shocked, I could hardly believe what you were telling me. But I knew you wouldn't lie about a thing like that. I didn't know what to think or who to talk to. Dad was out of town at a meeting, so I called Dr. Frank. You remember him, your pediatrician? He told me to move Ben's room and not say anything else about it. So that's what I did."

Just like that? That's it, the whole story?

Yes. I could see it. She loved us both, she was shocked into silence. And then advised into it. She had consulted the very best authority. It was 1963, before sexual abuse had come out of the closet, acquired a name.

It was advice that fit the times. Those were sweep-it-under-the-rug years and, in spite of our noisy conversations, we were a sweep-it-under-the-rug family.

Maybe this was okay for Ben, who didn't want to be reminded. Maybe it helped my mother, I don't know. But it was terrible for me not to talk, it nearly killed me. Because in those speechless days, I lost my sexual innocence and my brother at the same time.

Ben went off to college the next year, and I went to eighth grade swaddled in silence, knowing more than I could say about what everyone else was giggling about. I had to act normal, figure out how negotiate the sexual atmosphere of junior high, how to flirt with boys my own age. How to show just enough interest to get a boyfriend, but not give away so much that it ruined my reputation.

Ben married young. I got a fancy dress and a bouffant hairdo and danced at his wedding. After he graduated, he and his new wife, Claudia, joined the Peace Corps where they spent the next ten years in East Africa. We were all proud of the good work Ben was doing in a Third-World country. He wrote often, but we didn't see much of him except for occasional home leave. I couldn't shake the feeling that he was running away from something personal, not just that he liked his work. *But who knows? Don't put too much significance on what went on between us. He's probably forgotten the whole thing.*

The year I graduated from college my parents took us all on a trip to visit Ben and Claudia in Kenya. Our third day there Ben and I went for a drive alone; he was working on a project out in the bush he wanted to show me. He concentrated fiercely as he coaxed the jeep along a deeply rutted track, while I struggled with being carsick. Queasy, I knew I had to bring it up, finally.

"Ben, do you remember what happened between us when we were kids?" He never took his eyes from the path, didn't ask what I meant, *remember what?* He mumbled yes, but didn't say more.

That was the end of that. I couldn't say the next thing, ask the next question, whatever that was.

But some twenty years later, I had figured out what the next question was, with the help of a thoughtful, quiet therapist—the one before Dorothy—who used traditional talk therapy to help me figure out how to begin the conversation with my brother. It had taken an entire year, which Brenda called—accurately enough—

the Year-From-Hell. I was despondent, the way you are when you're forced to think about something you hoped to avoid forever. (It's obvious now, looking back, that I desperately needed to be on anti-depressants. But I never got a prescription, because when I broached the subject, Brenda screamed, "I'm not going to live with someone who's on drugs." Her ex-husband, Willy, had been a cocaine addict—she called him "that fucking junkie"—though what did that have to do with me? But because I was too weak to fight back, I just let it drop and went on being a zombie.)

I struggled to act like I was living in the present, where I was Sophie and Noah's mother, Brenda's partner, dealing with Thomas's problems. But, in fact, I was diminished. Thirteen again. In that black and white world, silence reigned. I lost a whole year and twenty-five pounds. No one could touch me, only my therapist could throw me a lifeline. My relationship with Brenda didn't end for two more years, but it certainly died that year.

At the culmination of the Year-from-Hell, I wrote Ben a letter telling him I needed to see him. We agreed to meet in a town halfway between our homes. It was the middle of January, on the cusp of my forty-first birthday; I decided this would be my birthday present. Arriving early at the designated place, I stepped out of the car into the cold, so he'd see me right away. But after a while, it got to be too cold, so I sat back down in the car to wait.

I waited.

And waited, until it turned as cold inside the car as out. *How long should I sit here?*

Now I understand what chilled to the bone really means. I'm going to look for Ben, I've been passive long enough. I walked briskly all around town, sticking my head into every restaurant and store, searching.

He wasn't anywhere. He never came.

How could he do this to me? Mind as numb as my body, I needed someone to tell me what to do. I called Brenda at work. Who put me on hold. Then, coming back to me, "I've got a long-distance call. Got to go, see you when you get home," and hung up.

I stood, holding a dead phone, disconnected, with snow swirling around my feet. Fifteen degrees out.

Blank. I didn't feel anything. I don't remember driving the icy road.

When I got back, the answering machine was blinking—6,6,6. Ben's disembodied voice, leaving bulletins with his location, sounding more panicked each time: "Where *are* you?"

I phoned him. "Where *were* you?"

"Hey, I was at the place we said we'd meet. Where were you?"

"No, you weren't. I waited for you there."

But obviously, one of us was wrong or maybe something else had gone wrong. Relieved that, at least, neither of us had stood the other up on purpose, we each apologized. *Maybe he's as nervous as I am?* We made another plan to meet.

A week later I started out on the same road. Alone in the car facing that drive a second time, not knowing what to expect, I thought about everyone who'd helped me get this far. Even though I wasn't all the way there yet—and I had to travel the rest of the way alone—I had gotten a lot of help. As I named those people to myself something happened that I wouldn't have believed if someone else told it to me.

The car slowly filled up with company. It was so unlikely, so magical, that all I could do was laugh. The first to arrive was my therapist who took the seat next to me. Always quiet, she didn't say much. Then, one by one, the Women's Group, who had listened to me agonize about the conversation I was driving to. Talkative and opinionated, they crowded into the backseat—there wasn't room to knit so they did that other thing they do—they talked and sympathized and cajoled—the car vibrated with their energy. I wasn't lonely or scared in that company.

This time Ben and I found each other.

What I remember about that day is walking. Icy footing, penetrating cold. When we greeted each other outside our cars with a tentative hug, Ben asked what I wanted to do. "Walk" I said, and so we did, all afternoon.

I started by telling him about therapy, about how I'd finally been able to tell someone what had happened between us, about how the not-talking had everything to do with how I had lived my life. About how I'd told our mother that the good advice she thought she'd gotten was bad for me.

And I asked him questions.

"Why did you do that to me? What could you possibly have been thinking? Have you ever told anyone?" And, finally, "How do you feel about yourself?"

He answered, slowly, choosing words carefully. When tears ran down his cheeks, he brushed them away impatiently. Normally I would have asked what he was feeling, what the tears were about. But I made myself not ask. I wanted the attention. *It's my turn.*

I know, this is the point where you want me to tell you what he said. But—think about it—what could he say?

"I'm sorry."

"I didn't mean to hurt you."

"I didn't understand sex, my own body, I got carried away."

"My desires drove me, you know those stupid jokes about boys, and men, 'thinking' with their dicks? Well, they're not so stupid. The jokes I mean, not the boys."

We both understood that nothing he said could undo what he'd done, no apology could take away the fact of how my sexual life began. But he did what he could. "None of it was your fault, Jesse, I'm the one completely to blame."

When I'd confronted our mother ten years before, she'd said many things. But the one that stuck with me was, "You were very beautiful and quite a sexy little thing." I don't think she *meant* to suggest I was responsible, but that's what I heard. *Maybe it was true that I'd been a sexy little thing. Did that make it my fault?*

Ben didn't say anything like that, not even a hint, not a whisper.

After we'd gotten through the really hard stuff, there was one more topic. About my being a lesbian. "When I found out I thought maybe I caused it," Ben said. "Then I thought some more about it and said to myself, 'Ben, don't be grandiose, you can't *make* someone into something they're not.'"

We laughed. At least he could still make fun of himself.

"And besides," I said, "being a lesbian is a gift in my life, so if you're responsible I would have you to thank."

We'd been walking for hours. We ate an early supper, we browsed the stores. Ben wanted to buy me something. I picked out a tiny, antique bottle made of Roman glass, excavated in Israel. This bottle, over 2000 years old, had a delicate rainbow patina. Something ancient, enduring.

"Is there anything at all I can do for you?" he asked.

Yes, there is. "I don't know why, but it makes me cry that I have so few memories of those years growing up together in Louisiana. Somehow, I've lost part of my own past. All I can remember clearly is riding wild horses, Betty-Baby catching snakes. What else is there?"

"That's easy," Ben said. "I'll write you a story about what you were like growing up. What we all did together, the gang of us." He paused. "You were really a spunky little kid," he said. "A real live wire."

And that's how the story about growing up in Louisiana got written. A gift from Ben, a piece of history that he gave back to me.

Somehow, the long walk in the cold redeemed us. We'd always been close. I had admired him with the adoration of a younger child; I could see now that he had admired me, too.

It seems almost unbelievable that *all* it took was that long talk for the past to recede, to return to where it belonged. Where it occupied just the right amount of space in my life, just part of it. Of course, that's not *all it took*, but when I was ready, talking seemed simple, and Ben met me half-way.

The story ends there. Almost.

There's one more thing. It's about transforming all that not-telling. The way intense pressure remakes coal into something entirely new, keeping secrets changed me. I became a professional listener. Already practiced at keeping quiet, listening to someone else's story came easily. Sensitized to the ways a placid surface can disguise turmoil, I could sense what was underneath.

When I would tell my clients I felt there was something important they hadn't been able to voice, their shocked expressions confirmed what I'd known intuitively. I'd heard the un-said.

I tried to make it safe enough for them to find words for their stories. Sometimes it was like coaxing a terrified animal out of hiding. Sometimes they could tell their stories out loud. Other times they would write them. It didn't matter; the telling was what was important.

Together we learned that how you label an experience, the name you give it, has everything to do with the story you tell *yourself*, about yourself. No one had to say anything directly for these women who carried their little girl-selves inside to believe it was *their fault*. That *it was no big deal*. They absorbed that from the world around them.

"She was asking for it."

"It was only messing around."

". . . just playing doctor."

"Boys will be boys."

Stories came pouring out, in whatever words the girl would have used if she'd been able to tell it when it happened to her.

"What Grampy did to me in the barn"—3 years old.

"Daddy woke me up in the night. Again"—4 1/2 years old.

"I asked my step-brother how babies were made and he showed me"—5 years old.

By the time her therapy was complete, she'd integrated the little girl and together they understood that she hadn't been *asking for* anything. That she'd been manipulated, molested, violated, sexually abused. That her anger and hurt made sense.

This is what I learned from all those years of not-talking and then telling *my* story, all those years of listening while other women told theirs. Telling helps. If you can find a person who can hear you. It could be a therapist, or a mother, or a lover. Or the people in your survivors' support group. For me, it helped most to tell the person who hurt me, and he listened to every word I said. Which was practically heroic.

And it helped to understand that what happened is not nothing, but it doesn't have to be everything either.

23

Like Air

"SHE WAS LIKE AIR." The woman, a therapist with the unlikely name of Sage, paused, embarrassed, almost stammering, trying to pin down something so ephemeral. "Everywhere. Essential." Puny words would never be adequate to express her soaring emotions. She stared into her past, looking like she might try one more time to explain. But didn't. It was either completely obvious, or so unique and complicated, that no one who wasn't her would ever really understand. Or approve.

The story she didn't tell: She and Anna had a circumscribed relationship for a couple of years, defined by roles and boundaries. The way they came together had been unplanned and random, and their beginning was tumultuous.

Sage had been the therapist; the air-like one, Anna, the client. They encountered each other at the end of Anna's decade of trouble, marked by binges, hospitalizations, and despair. It was rough going at first, so difficult that they each thought of abandoning the work before them. Anna was despondent, believing that she was beyond help. Sage was wary of a client so driven, possessed, in fact, by personal demons. *Maybe exorcism would be more effective than*

traditional talk therapy? But they were both fighters, and once having committed to the work, they persevered, calling it "slogging through the swamp." By the time they terminated, Anna's sobriety was integrated into her life, and she was ready to move on.

As they grew to know each other, they realized that they'd stumbled onto unanticipated common ground. They recognized each other. Which was odd since on the surface they were from what seemed like opposite worlds, with histories so unlike, that the familiar feeling was inexplicable. They noticed this out loud in one session, but still they hugged the boundaries.

Anna had lived the public life of a professional athlete. She'd learned about herself by running up mountains with a pack of rocks on her back, and by sitting in the back of some room in countless church basements, a silent participant during AA meetings. She didn't trust words to capture her skittering feelings.

Sage lived a sedentary life; a listener and a talker, a wordsmith, she was newly engaged in reclaiming her Jewish roots. But they perceived something in the other, something that beckoned, even though they couldn't name it. And as they talked on, they laughed about how many times their lives had *almost* intersected. "This incarnation," as they said, was the one they were living now, but there were so many other times where their paths almost crossed.

When Anna terminated therapy, they shyly acknowledged that they might miss seeing each other. Then they shook hands and each went on with her life. Anna moved north, building a house and barn on a hillside. She created gardens, and filled the barn with animals to tend and to love, reinventing herself as a farmer. Sage stayed put, continuing to see clients and taking care of her children. Maybe they missed each other a bit more than they had anticipated, but their lives were full. They exchanged a couple of postcards just to stay in touch, but after a while even that stopped, and they lost contact.

But then one November, there was the annual conference that brought together all elements of the gay community in their rural state. People came out of the hills—literally—to see one another and to be seen. The conference was really just an excuse to get together, to be visible after long seasons of invisibility.

Sage always looked forward to this gathering: the sessions, the music, the carnival-like atmosphere. She arrived early just to get an eyeful of who'd come out of the hills. And there was Anna. They went for coffee and caught up on what they'd each been doing, attended the morning session together, walked downtown for lunch. They'd never taken a walk together, or shared a meal, but somehow it felt perfectly natural. Like this was something they'd been doing their entire lives.

Back at the conference the afternoon session was about Nazi persecution of homosexuals. Slides projected gigantic images of gaunt men in prison stripes marked by pink triangles. Sage looked as long as she could, and then wordlessly dropped her head down on the desk. Anna's light touch on her back let her know that when she found the courage to look again there would be something beyond those photographs.

A fierce, snowy wind snapped around them when they hugged a quick goodbye in the parking lot. That hug changed them. Through their heavy coats they both felt heat, heat that would alter everything, forcing them to embrace a new future. It seemed impossibly magical, but that day, in that snow-filled moment, they became a couple. They both knew it.

And both tried fiercely to ignore it by focusing harder on their individual lives, trying to forestall a future so fraught, so impossible, they could not even consider it. It took several months; they talked on the phone, met in towns where no one knew them, they took long walks in the snow. One day Anna was humming, and Jesse joined in with the words.

> Sit by my side, come as close as the air,
> share in a memory of gray, and wander in my words,
> and dream about the pictures that I play,
> of changes.

Without planning, one song merging into the next, they sang through the entire repertoire of Ian and Sylvia's hits. Anna had been raised on classical music, but the first folk songs she learned when she left her parents' house were those tunes. Jesse knew the words.

"We were singing the same songs all those years ago." Something that insignificant sealed their togetherness. They sang their way into a new reality.

As a therapist, Sage had been trained in the traditional model. She knew about professional boundaries: *Never, ever get involved with a patient.* Everything in her professional life was at stake. Could she try to convince herself that this was a unique situation with extenuating circumstances? Certainly it was true that there was no coercion or abuse of power involved. Anna was not a young woman, not under the powerful sway of an older, wiser therapist, she'd been out of therapy for some time. Blah, blah, blah.

But even though she tried, no amount of self-talk convinced her that it would be ethical for her to continue working as a therapist if she became involved with Anna. Her personal integrity, *doing the right thing*, had always been a cornerstone of her identity. Maybe this was her comeuppance—her mother might have suggested this—for being judgmental of other people, assuming that the right choice was always obvious. It had taken Anna for her to understand that sometimes decisions aren't so simple.

She agonized, wordlessly, struggling to push the turmoil into a corner where it wouldn't damage her everyday life. She turned Anna into a secret. Until she couldn't, because she was so miserable she could barely think of anything else, which forced her to confront the reality that she'd better talk to someone, and soon.

She started with friends, then colleagues. Everyone had a point of view:

"You can make this work. There's nothing wrong with what you're doing. Anna had terminated therapy before you ever even considered getting involved. You haven't done anything unethical."

"You're a gifted therapist. You can't quit. Think of your other clients, and how much they still need you."

"This is what you've done for twenty-eight years. What other work can you possibly do?"

And, finally: "Don't blame Anna if you decide to close your practice. You've been talking about quitting for at least two years, because of the hearing thing."

She talked to her own therapist who, though unconventional herself, toed the line on this boundary, and advised against getting involved with a former client.

Her oldest friend always had her best interests in mind: "It seems pretty dicey to me. I wonder how you'll feel about yourself later if you do get involved with her. And what if it doesn't work out?"

Her brother: "I'm worried about the ethical issues. You'd be risking your career for a relationship you're not sure of."

Every point was valid and worth considering, even when they contradicted each other. Each focused of a different facet of the dilemma, leaving Sage with what she'd known even before she asked. This decision was hers alone.

The one person Sage had avoided telling was her closest professional colleague. She put it off until she couldn't *not* say something. The friend was adamant. "I can't maintain contact with you after what you've done." *Is she worried about sullying her own professional reputation by associating with me?* Somehow this was exactly what Sage had dreaded hearing. Unwilling to let this precious relationship go without a fight, she wrote and called, but her friend was gone.

Those were the outside opinions. Adding to the din were the clamoring interior voices, arguing one position, then another:

Those rules are there for a reason. They make it safe for both client and therapist to engage in intimate conversation without worrying that it will turn into something else.

You've believed in these boundaries your entire professional life. Why are you risking your career now?

Those ethics are valuable and important, but they won't put a hand on your back when you need it most.

And finally, simply, *It's your life. Don't ask other people. Make your own damn decision.*

Eventually she came up with an analogy that she could live with: if a priest, having taken vows of celibacy, leaves the priesthood when he falls in love with someone, that doesn't negate his previous commitment. He honored his vows. Until he couldn't. Somehow this helped.

Sage closed her practice after a year of trying to squeeze professional ethics and love into a space where they could co-exist. She would not deny this love which offered her a future—unknown, to be sure—but promising surprises and new joy.

There were losses: the loss of how she thought of herself (*I'm a therapist*), the lost friendship. Those hurt. Other changes—not being so judgmental and critical—were for the better.

And always there was Anna.

"I realized I felt about her the way some people feel about God," Sage went on with her story, making herself put it into words. "Not to be grandiose but, she was everywhere, surrounding me."

You probably know by now that I'm Sage—I'd changed my name during the reject-the-patriarchy-let's-name-ourselves-for-herbs '70s. Now I'm just Jesse again. This is the story about my decision. About losses and love. About honoring vows until you can't. And about making new vows that will endure.

We're celebrating five years together, Anna and I.

I just wanted to tell you.

24

Wife?

"Do you, Jesse, take Anna to be your beloved wife?"
"I do."
"Do you, Anna, take Jesse to be your beloved wife?"
"I do."
Crowd breaks into wild applause, shouting *Mazel Tov!*
Cut. Cut! Wait. I never said that.
I know I never said it, because I'd never been allowed to say it. And when I finally could, I'd lost the desire.
Never *wife*.

Our wedding, like every wedding, carried freight, some of it typical and some unique, because we were two women marrying. "Joining in Civil Union" was the term permitted, we couldn't legally *marry*. The M word was reserved exclusively for "one man and one woman." (*One? What about divorce?* I hear you saying.)

While the event itself wasn't entirely unique, the coverage certainly was. Because while most couples announce their marriage in the society pages of their local newspaper, the story about our ceremony appeared on the front page of *The Washington Post*, complete with color photographs of the smiling brides.

How did such a private celebration become a media event?

At first it seemed simple. Our decision to allow Helen, a reporter who worked for the *Post*, to write a human-interest article about our wedding practically made itself. Anna and Helen were part-time neighbors, since Helen had been coming to unwind from the demands of city life at a house on the dirt road where Anna lived. They talked politics outside the barn, they shared local gossip and as time went on, Anna introduced Helen to the finer points of the dairy goat business. So you can imagine how pleased we were when Helen dropped us a note to let us know she'd landed the assignment to "put a human face" on civil unions. Could she interview us? When she heard a couple of months later that we were getting married, she grabbed the opportunity—could she base her article on our civil union? Such an ally.

This question presented itself during final wedding preparations—something else to consider, requiring us to take a break from deciding whether the catering staff should wear traditional black and white or casual attire, whether the band should play 60's Rock 'n' Roll or something less raucous?—important questions like that—to talk it over. How would it feel to invite a public we'd never meet to share our wedding with us?

Well, why not? Who could humanize the story better than Helen who knew us and appreciated our lives? Ultimately, it was the phrase "putting a human face on it" that swayed us. A cliché maybe, but it prompted our decision.

Well, we made the paper all right. There we are on the bottom of page one! a beautiful color photograph of Anna and me with our arms around each other, smiling directly into the eye of the camera. *We look great!, they chose a good photo, didn't they?*—then I froze as I glanced at the headline: SAME-SEX UNION DIVIDES SMALL VERMONT COMMUNITY. I stared at those words. "*DIVIDES*"? *What are they talking about?*

It wasn't like that. That's not what happened. Noah, world-weary at sixteen, waited for my protests to subside before patiently informing me, "Mom, everyone and her cousin has a happy wedding. That's not *news*. There's got to be some angle."

Angle. Wasn't two women getting married enough of an angle? Wasn't the fact that William Sloane Coffin—weakened by a stroke but still fighting the good fight at eighty—performed the ceremony, wasn't that enough of an angle? Weren't the one hundred guests, a crowd that stretched from three months old to ninety-three, all of our brothers and sisters; my father and stepmother; other friends and family who traveled from as far away as California to stand with us on this Vermont hillside, weren't they an angle?

The article was somber and dark, the women besieged. A cloud of controversy hung ominously over them as they struggled to express their love in a ceremony that aped a *real* wedding.

How did someone who knew us, who presented herself as a supportive ally, get it completely wrong? The newspaper account of our wedding was so different from my experience that, for a moment, I wondered if Helen was actually writing about some other event. I know reality can be subjective, but this was an out-and-out distortion.

Furious, I sought relief in tearing the article apart, line-by-line, word-by-inaccurate-word, starting with the implication that Anna is a bigot who decides whether to tell the truth based on appearances:

> "'I'm not telling that tent guy I'm marrying another woman,' says Anna Rosewood . . . she's judging by what she sees through the window: big arms, shaved head and a scar . . . The drama—won't tell him, will tell him—repeats that morning . . . Now that Rosewood has decided to put up a white tent the whole world can see, nearly every encounter is making her nervous."

Anna was nervous all right, but I can tell you that what was making her anxious wasn't the tent man. We'd divided responsibilities for our wedding based on who was good at what: I'd arranged the catering, so I was focused on whether the food would be as delectable as it sounded on paper. Anna, the expert gardener, was responsible for the lawns and grounds of her hillside farm. She was focused on whether the grass she'd mowed, edges clipped with special shears, and the flower gardens she'd lovingly tended, offered a visual feast for our guests about to drive up the hill.

> "The fight over gay civil unions used to be waged among strangers... but now as Rosewood and hundreds of others begin to exercise the new rights, it's getting more intimate, played out on front lawns, neighbor to neighbor."

Part of that, at least, was true. We were playing it out on our front lawn, Anna did invite neighbors. And they came: Dusty, the dairyman from the next farm over, arrived wearing his usual outfit, tight brown T-shirt stretched over his enormous belly. He was escorting his wife Matilda and mother, Polly, who came up to his chest. He embraced Anna, saying, "Now I guess I'll have to take your name out of my little black book" winking at me. Marybelle, at ninety-three our oldest guest, had grown up on this farm in the early 1900s. She lived in California now, and had traveled the farthest—emotionally and geographically—to celebrate with us.

Carla, Maggie, Julia, Lizanne—the Women's Group—arrived together, walking up the long driveway accompanied by spouses, boyfriends, and children. These women had heard in exquisite detail every struggle and joy on the way to this wedding day.

Family arrived: our brothers and sisters with wives and husbands, cousins, nephews, nieces, babies. My eighty-year-old father remembered Bill Coffin from when they met at a SANE/FREEZE rally thirty years before. Aunt Judith, whose life as a closeted lesbian had almost crushed her, clutched me so tightly she squeezed the breath out of me. "I never thought I'd live long enough to see this." I could only glimpse what she'd barely survived.

As you know, Anna and I had each lived an entire history before we became a couple. Honoring our individual pasts, embracing our future together, we had gathered people we loved from every part of our lives. A grab bag of past and present, sharing one common denominator: everyone was here to celebrate.

We'd designed a ceremony to embrace our different backgrounds. I wanted Jewish tradition and group singing. Anna needed classical music; she'd arranged for a cello and piano duo. The spirit of Anna's parents, long gone, inhabited those moments before the ceremony as we sat together listening to Bach and Tchaikovsky. Music brought the presence of their beloved parents to our celebration. My arm around Anna, I glanced over at her sisters and brother, who were all weeping. They knew who was being honored.

After the concert, we walked behind the *chuppa* to a circle of maple trees. We were a long line: kids leading the way, old women with walkers maneuvered cautiously down the stony driveway. A hundred people spread out makes a slow procession. Anna's goats gamboled and pranced along escorting us, delighted that they'd been included in the festivities.

The *chuppa* is traditionally made of the Jewish groom's prayer shawl, but since there wasn't a groom, I'd asked Noah if we could use his. The sixteen-year-old's version of *yes* was not effusive, but I could tell he knew he was making a special contribution. We had stretched the *tallit* between four hand-cut sticks from Anna's woods, another melding of two traditions. The *chuppa* holders, Noah, Sophie, Anna's sister Gerri and niece, Barbara, took their responsibilities seriously, extending their arms straight up. Because if they relaxed their grip, the *chuppa* sagged down, draping Bill Coffin's white head.

We arrived under the trees, maple leaves making a canopy above our *chuppa*. The guests sat in a semicircle on folding wooden chairs, facing us, looking out over rolling hills. Anna and I stood holding hands under the *tallit*.

But that's not what subscribers to the *Post* read over their morning coffee. They didn't hear the concert, didn't meet our family or any of our friends. They met the Johnsons:

> "In this standoff, Cabot turns out to be a perfect stage—
> not upscale like the nearby skiing resorts at Stowe but
> headed that way. Drive the one-mile stretch of Joseph's

> Pond Road... and you'll pass, on your left, the Johnsons, who politely declined an invitation to the ceremony because, 'We believe in the word of God.'"

That's true, they did say that. And since that's what they believe, thank God they didn't come. But drive a half-mile the other direction and you'll pass, on your right, a biracial lesbian couple who raise sheep, and two houses down, a gay man who's a professional bird carver.

> "Before Silverman arrives, Rosewood is remembering her first image of lesbians: two women who lived in the 'haunted house' deep in the woods near her childhood home. One day someone knocked on their door and found them dead, one of alcohol poisoning, the other of a self-inflicted gunshot wound. Somehow Anna deduced that this would be your natural end if you were a farm lesbian and preferred to be around girls."

Farm lesbian?

> "She kept quiet, or closeted as they say now. For forty years. Fumbling through silly relationships with men and destructive fixations on women. Throwing her energy into her career as a professional runner and drinking, lots of drinking."

Yes, there had been a lot of drinking. But how was this relevant to our wedding? If we'd known that the article would air a troubled past, we would never have even considered it. Maybe we were naive, but we never entertained the possibility that one angle would be Anna's personal struggle. Why would we? This wasn't *The National Enquirer*, after all.

We had thought our-friend-the-reporter was writing about one subject, but she was searching for something dramatic to capture an audience. Something sensational: *Famous athlete, after years of struggling with her lesbianism and alcoholism, finally emerges. Victorious!* The human face we'd thought we were showing wasn't exciting enough for the newspaper.

And there's something else: I was embarrassed to admit that it bothered me, because I most *definitely* did not want to be overexposed the way Anna was. But *I* was invisible. Like a photograph where the foreground is in sharp focus, but the background fades into shadow, insignificant. Was Anna the only one getting married? Or just the only famous one? Good thing they printed a photograph so you could see the two of us together, because you sure couldn't tell from the text.

Here's how I made my appearance. Regina Johnson got to speak her piece. I'm the silent "partner."

> "'Anna's partner has a little girl, named Sophie I think. It's her I worry about,' says Regina Johnson. 'I'm afraid she's going to be swayed, you know, taught to live that way. And I'd hate to see her hurt.'"

"Taught to live that way." *We appreciate your concern for Sophie's well-being, Regina. Now if you'll just deal with your own prejudices, Sophie won't be hurt by you.*

> "'My feeling is it's her business, but if we went to the wedding, or whatever they call it, we would be approving it,' says Donald Johnson. 'I believe in God's word, and that's what I wrote her in the reply note. But we're still going to be friends.'
>
> 'Yes, she's a very nice girl,' adds Regina. 'They are good people. Very good people.'"

Yes, Donald, they call it a wedding.

> "If truth be told, he's not really very religious, Donald Johnson says, if that means you go to church every Sunday and quote the Bible by heart. But what bothers him is the change coming so quickly, stealing a state and a way of being he has known all his life."

Now that I think about it, "stealing the state" is indeed a frightening prospect. If that were the case, I might understand why Donald was upset. But how my wedding *steals the state*—that's more power than I ever knew I had.

But let's address what's really upsetting Donald, the loss of "a way of being he has known all his life."

The way of being *I've* known all my life is hiding, fear, denying who I love, being told that I'm sick or a sinner. I'm sorry Mr. Johnson has to face changes, faster than he wanted, so I can have the same rights he has. The right to celebrate my love in the daylight.

> "It's not as if he didn't know who was gay in town, but they used to keep 'very quiet.' 'Now, you're supposed to celebrate . . . Now it's right there near the Wedding Section, a picture of Jen and Susie or whatever, and that ain't right. It's too open.'"

Oh, my God, right near the Wedding Section! But at least Mr. Johnson got something right. Now you're supposed to celebrate.

This next part is wrong geographically, since these guys, the Rogers brothers, live too far off the road to see any traffic going by. But they, too, have their say:

> "By 2:30 p.m., the traffic gets heavy as cars make their way up to Rosewood's house. The Rogers brothers watch it all from the trailer they use as a hunting lodge, wondering what's going on. They helped their neighbor put up his 'Take Back Vermont' sign just across from their trailer . . . but they want to emphasize that they too are good neighbors . . . 'If a gay guy wants to come hunting with us, that's all right,' offers Darryl Rogers. 'But he has to be tough, not a pansy-ass.'"

That's pansy. Or candy-ass. But never, never pansy-ass (you dumb redneck).

> "Polly Chamberlain, 71, has lived and milked cows here most of her life. When she was a school girl, she never knew the word, 'gay' except, of course, to mean happy she explains . . . cutting poppy seeds from her garden, her boots still muddy from morning chores at the barn . . . Later she thought about it and figured, 'you can accept it or fight it. But I've got no fight left in me.' . . . So she wrote

this reply to Rosewood and Silverman: 'I will come to the wedding. Anna is a good friend and a good neighbor. Everyone is the same no matter who they marry. The best to you both.'"

Divides a small community? Sounds like our wedding is giving people in town the chance to rethink old prejudices. The headline should be, CIVIL UNION OFFERS SMALL TOWN OPPORTUNITY TO REPAIR ITSELF. That would have been closer to the truth.

"Joan Solomon leads the guests in a group chant in Hebrew. Then William Sloane Coffin talks about true love, forgiveness, homophobia, and his friends' bravery in 'helping millions of others create a world in which cruelty is more of the exception than the rule.'"

Finally the touching conclusion, the human face.

"'Anna, will you have this woman to be your beloved wife?' Coffin asks.
'Yes, I will.'
Then the echo: 'Yes, I will.'
And they hug like old friends."

The final ritual of a Jewish wedding is the moment the groom stomps on a glass, shattering it. But, of course, we each insisted on our own glass. So two glasses smashed, then clapping and cheers of *Mazel Tov*!

We had agreed that we would hold hands and run up to the house for some private time before joining the party. But, plans being what they are, Anna dropped my hand, and turned back to embrace Bill, who had blessed us with his presence, and to kiss Sophie and the other *chuppa* holders, who were just now lowering their trembling arms.

She caught up with me part way up the hill. We had an ecstatic escort all the way along the fence line to the house, Anna's goats frolicking and calling. Two shattered glasses, goat escorts: the birth of a new tradition.

The food was delicious. Guests, old and young, loved the rock 'n' roll music and danced the night away. The dancing chair, another tradition, was modified as Anna and I were both hoisted into the air by the strongest men and danced around to a raucous rendition of *Hava Na Gila*. Anna, ever the athlete, loved it, bouncing up and down and shrieking in time to the music. I was terrified and couldn't wait to be delivered back to the ground. Anna could've bounced on her chair all night.

That's what really happened.

But back to the article: "They hug like old friends." Can you imagine describing any heterosexual wedding like that? So much for romance. Goodbye, sexuality. Evidently *old friends* is reserved for middle-aged lesbians who aren't supposed to celebrate (or even acknowledge?) their passion.

And finally that freighted word, *wife*. That's not really such a terrible word, you say. And you're right. Unless it's been denied you an entire lifetime, long enough to absorb weighty connotations like *belonging to*, like man and *wife*, like *wifely duties*. I don't object to anyone else using it—I'm a tolerant person—but it could never describe me.

If not *wife*, what then?

1. lover (too sexual)
2. significant other (too '70s)
3. partner (too business-like)
4. sweetie (too cute)
5. spouse (too distant)
6. beloved (too schmaltzy)

We'll work on finding a term that fits. For now, it's Anna, just Anna.

Meanwhile, how could she do this to us, our friendly-neighbor-the-reporter? We had welcomed her, opened our private world, and she'd used us. Never in a million years would we have offered our wedding as a vehicle for ignorance and hate.

Since Anna was closer to Helen she had more reason to try to maintain the relationship. She read the article through just once. I read it over and over, raging—VIOLATED, EXPOSED,

BETRAYED—trying my damnedest to engage Anna. She listened, but refused to re-read the article.

Married now, I remembered that famous quote from Kahlil Gibran:

> Let there be spaces in your togetherness,
> And let the winds of the heavens dance between you . . .
> and stand together yet not too near together:
> For the pillars of the temple stand apart,
> And the oak tree and the cypress grow not in
> each other's shadow.

The winds of heaven were dancing now. And no one was standing in anyone's shadow.

But for all my fuming, it was Anna who finally summed it up best by telling me the story of Helen's wedding, which had been celebrated two years earlier at the house down the road. Family had flown in from Washington and New York, then driven into Vermont hill country, where they arrived looking shell-shocked, convinced they were in the hinterlands, worried they might never find their way home to civilization. Helen and the groom, Daniel, had a traditional Jewish wedding, complete with *chuppa*, an imported rabbi and elaborate Kosher spread. Uninvited neighbors drove by, staring at the fancy cars, the men in yarmulkes, the ritual canopy. These were neighbors who didn't know they knew a Jew.

So Helen, how would you have felt if some reporter had interviewed those neighbors, soliciting their opinion about the skull caps and Hebrew chanting? Inviting them to give voice to their dark fears about Jews?

When we called Helen she'd been eagerly waiting to hear from us, anticipating how much we'd just love the article. She sputtered, completely taken aback as Anna patiently explained what the problem was.

I couldn't stand all this polite constraint and wrestled the phone away. Because I was on the verge of exploding. "Helen, how could you do that to us? What were you thinking?"

"What do you mean?"

"Look, we invited you to our wedding, which is just about as personal as you can get. How could you say those things?"

"What are you talking about? Everything I wrote was absolutely true."

"From your perspective, maybe. But you got the tone all wrong."

"I wrote what I saw, and quoted exactly what people said to me. There wasn't anything inaccurate in that article."

"But I'm telling you the tone distorted the entire day. You made it sound like we were under siege and that the neighbors were up in arms, and you know perfectly well that's not what it was like."

"Why are you harping on tone? I got the facts right, like I just said."

"You're a journalist, Helen. You know facts can be manipulated to create whatever impression you want. Look at how you framed the story, starting with that headline. The angle you took distorted the reality of our wedding day."

"I can hear you're upset, Jesse. Let me tell you what happened on my end."

"Do I want to hear this? Our wedding divided the community? 'The word of God . . . taught to live *that* way.' Come on, Helen, you invited the neighbors to give voice to prejudice and hate for the sake of your story. It certainly wasn't *our* story."

"Will you stop talking long enough for me to tell my side? I showed the first version to my editors. They said it was too long and told me to cut some descriptive stuff and add more context. That's when I went out and got those quotes from neighbors. But their main complaint was that you two looked too good. That you were heroes of your own story."

"So what? Maybe we did look good. Isn't that what every bride wants on her wedding day? After all the fear, all the hiding, what's wrong with taking center stage? You said you'd *put a human face* on civil unions, which is why we agreed to let you write the story in the first place. You put a face on us all right. It's just not a face I'd recognize as mine."

I'd exhausted myself, and it was obvious Helen had stopped listening. I imagined her holding the phone away from her ear, letting me go on and on. But I had to, just had to, say one last thing. "Helen, you know we never said 'wife.'"

It was not possible. We could be heroes, maybe. But never wives.

25

Next of Kin

AFTER ALL THOSE YEARS of constant vigilance, it's a relief to let down your guard. Dropping that lifelong, protective armor, everything feels so much lighter and somehow safer. After all, Anna and I got married four years ago this September. You've heard all about our ceremony, the *chuppa*, the two smashed glasses, the gamboling goats. That article in *The Washington Post* was an outrage, but after we'd written our letter to the editor protesting the distortions in the story, we'd moved on, reveling in our newfound status as married people. Everything was wonderful, right?

Right.

Anna and I celebrated by sharing our news, deciding to assume people would be happy for us. After a lifetime of hiding, we told *everyone*, from the guys at the hardware store to Sophie's teachers. Mostly our announcement was met with smiles and congratulations, just like any other marriage. Sometimes there was an awkward silence, but we just forged ahead. What could anyone say? It was legal. We were married (well, civil-unionized, but we called ourselves married).

But questions about how *real* our marriage is just wouldn't go away, even though we've tried to fit in, make ourselves as "normal" as two middle-aged, quirky lesbians can be.

We'd been in the newspaper, we'd told everyone, so I was caught off guard when my marriage lost its status in the most unanticipated circumstance, my mammogram appointment. For many women this may be a slightly unpleasant but otherwise straightforward procedure, but it's freighted for me, as you can imagine, remembering that my mother died young from breast cancer. In fact, this year I am the age she was when she was diagnosed, just fifty-three. (Which didn't seem so young then, but feels positively youthful now.)

Anna and I have this discussion twice a year, " Do you want me to come with you to the appointment?" Every time I ask myself, *Will it be better if I go alone and try to ignore the emotional baggage? Can I convince myself, it's fine, no big deal, just another appointment? Or would it be better to have Anna come, so when I emerge from the examining room she'll be sitting right there, reading a magazine, waiting for me?*

It's always the same conversation. Sometimes I decide one way, sometimes the other. This year I decided to go alone.

I got to the hospital early, because I like to have time to check in without rushing. I love this community hospital, it's so small and intimate. It's right across the state line in New Hampshire, but so close everyone considers it our local hospital. The technician who does the mammogram seems to really care when she squeezes so hard it hurts, apologizing as she explains that she has to squeeze even harder, and tells you to hold your breath.

I know the routine at the appointment desk: name, address, insurance, next of kin . . . The young woman stared at the computer screen while she asked the questions, verifying my information. No changes, everything's the same.

"Next of kin—Anna? Is this your sister?"

"No, she's my spouse." Pause. *Breathe.* "We're married."

"What? Oh. I understand. I get what you're saying. Uh, I'm really sorry to have to tell you this, I don't agree, you know, but I don't think we can use her name. The State doesn't allow it."

"But I've always listed her as next of kin. And now it's legal."

"I know. I'm really sorry. They must have assumed she was your sister. I'm in the same situation; I have a daughter with the man I've lived with for ten years, but I can't list him as next of kin. Even though he knows my wishes better than anyone in my family, I have to use my aunt."

She paused, stuck. "But wait a minute, I'll ask my supervisor."

She called over the supervisor, a slightly older woman. They conferred, and then the supervisor turned to me. "We asked the lawyer about this last time it came up and he checked with the State. We can't use your woman partner. It's the law. If you die at the hospital, we can't release your body to anybody but your next of kin. Don't you have someone else who you can list?"

"You mean, if they squeeze too hard and I die during my mammogram you can't release my body?" Thinking a joke might help.

"No."

Well, of course, I have other people I can list. I could give you my eighty-two-year old father's name. Sophie's thirteen, so she's out of the question, but Noah just turned eighteen. That'd really be fun for him to collect my body.

"I'm really upset. But I'm not mad at you," I said, hoping to defuse the situation. "But I won't give you any other name if you won't take Anna's. If she were a man and we were married, she'd be my next of kin, right? She's my legal spouse. If you won't take her name, I won't give you a name."

The clerk nodded, the supervisor nodded, and with one click the clerk erased Anna off the screen. I watched as her name disappeared.

You can keep my damn body, I thought, as I turned away and headed down the hall toward Radiology.

26

Blessing

WHEN THE LETTER ARRIVED, it was mixed in with the usual mail: bills, catalogs, and appeals for money from various do-good groups. A letter from the synagogue didn't seem out of the ordinary since Sophie goes to religious school there twice a week to prepare for her bat mitzvah, so they're always sending me something. Sometimes these letters are really a bill, or an announcement of a klezmer band or some other event worth noting in our part of northern New England. There's not much Jewish going on here, except during the High Holidays when Jews come flooding out of the hills, and it's astonishing how many of us really live here. Then Yom Kippur comes and goes, and everything's back to normal. The fifteen or so regulars have Shabbat services all to themselves.

So when I opened the envelope I wasn't paying much attention. But this wasn't a bill. Inside was an *aliyah* invitation. My spouse and I were being given the honor of reciting blessing before and after the Torah reading. The time of our *aliyah* was already set, the fifth slot on the first morning of Rosh Hashanah. All that was needed was my Hebrew name, the Hebrew names of my mother and father, my spouse's Hebrew name and the Hebrew names of my spouse's mother and father.

Just fill in the blanks. *Oh, no. Now what do I do?*

The last time I'd given an *aliyah* I'd had to study those six lines for weeks, even though I was reading the transliteration, not even Hebrew. Because I can't read Hebrew. And that time someone had sung the blessing with me. Since then, every time I was invited to come to the *bimah*, I always declined. The last time I demurred the rabbi said sweetly, "You're supposed to accept, it's an honor," but I remained resolute.

No one alive knew the weight of this simple honor.

The obstacles to accepting the *aliyah* seemed endless: I don't have a Hebrew name, my mother and father didn't have Hebrew names, my spouse isn't Jewish. And she's a woman. (We can assume her parents didn't have Hebrew names either, but that seemed the least of our troubles.) And the rabbi at this synagogue refused to marry us, even after civil unions became legal in Vermont. (I never did know whether this was because we were lesbians or because ours would have been a mixed marriage.) My hurt and outrage led me to boycott services—which wasn't really so hard since I'd lived a lifetime without going to synagogue—but after a year, I realized that I missed it. I'd returned to the site of the insult, because it was the only synagogue in town.

Now, suddenly, Anna and I were being given an *aliyah* on one of the holiest days of the year. How was I supposed to understand this?

I mulled over the invitation for a week, not mentioning it to Anna because I wanted to sort out my own feelings. When I realized I was going around in circles, that I needed more information, I called the president of the congregation. Did they really mean to include Anna? Did they know she wasn't Jewish? Maybe I should sing the blessing with Sophie and Noah, who have the distinct advantage of reading Hebrew.

Perhaps I was hoping that by telling the president these things I'd get off the hook. Maybe she didn't realize we were a lesbian couple, and once she knew, she'd retract the offer. Then I could be righteously angry, all over again, about ubiquitous, rampant homophobia.

But, no, the president cheerfully assured me that Anna and I were both being honored as Sophie's parents. We could both go up on the *bimah,* although Anna could not sing the blessing because she's not Jewish. Not having a Hebrew name wasn't a problem at all, I could just use my English name. Same for Anna.

Oh, no. Now what?

What's the big deal? you might be asking yourself. You're Jewish, aren't you? Just go up there and recite the damn thing. What could be so hard about that?

Well, let me tell you.

Yes, I was born Jewish. In fact, as you already know, my Grandfather Solomon was a prominent Reform rabbi, and my grandmother Esther had been a well-known Jewish author. In spite of which, I never stepped inside a synagogue until I was thirteen. I wanted to go, I'd bugged my mother about it for a whole year. She never really said no, it just never happened. Until finally, one Sunday, without preamble, she drove me to the local synagogue, walked me in to meet the rabbi and religious school director, and left as soon as she possibly could without seeming rude. I was alone in a Conservative *shul* with a group of teenagers who all seemed to be best friends, and who could sing every one of the Hebrew prayers. What could I do? I was thirteen, I didn't know a single kid there. I certainly wasn't going to be able to study hard or fast enough to be ready for my bat mitzvah. (Thinking back on it now, I'm not even sure that synagogue celebrated bat mitzvahs in 1963. But I didn't even know that.) I stayed as long as I could stand it, but I only lasted a few weeks. Then, I stopped asking my mother to drive me to the synagogue. Ashamed of how far behind I was, I regretted the experiment in searching for my Jewish roots.

That was the year before my grandfather, the famous rabbi, came to live with us. Grandmother Esther had died several years before, and now my father and Aunt Judith had determined that Grandfather Solomon couldn't live on his own any longer. Though Aunt Judith lived in Brooklyn in the heart of a flourishing Jewish community, she was a closeted lesbian, sharing a one-bedroom apartment with her lover. So she was out. Our home was the other option, and though it wasn't New York, we had just moved to a city with a sizable Jewish population. It all made sense, except for one thing; my mother didn't like my grandfather. She walked out of rooms he walked into, her face pinched. "Too goddamn intellectual," she muttered, just out of my grandfather's earshot. "The only thing those Silvermans think about is books and politics. They don't care about people one iota." When Grandfather Solomon insisted on teaching five-year-old Isaac to play chess—only to checkmate him every time—she nodded grimly as if that just proved her point.

My father was oblivious to the problem, leaving family matters in my mother's capable hands. But her intense dislike, my father's indifference, and my grandfather's ignorance of what was swirling around him made for a toxic mix. The saving grace for Grandfather Solomon was supposed to be me, with my Jewish yearnings. Except no one told me.

After my grandfather had been with us a couple of weeks, early one Saturday morning he suggested that we go to Shabbat services together. I wasn't sure what to wear, but threw on an outfit I thought suitably conservative. My father drove, dropping us off at the front door. As we stepped inside, Grandfather Solomon was welcomed enthusiastically by the young rabbi who clasped both his hands, nodding reverentially at every word the old man said, as if he were a visiting dignitary. Which he was. I just didn't know it. No one I knew had ever treated my grandfather like that. I saw at him a little differently out of the corner of my eye.

The rabbi escorted us to our seats in the front row and the service began. Guess what? My grandfather was fluent in Biblical Hebrew, knew all the prayers by heart, singing them enthusiastically and loudly. But, the old man couldn't carry a tune. I squirmed in my seat, pretending we weren't related, which was hard because I'd just been welcomed as the granddaughter of the distinguished rabbi.

But something happened to me that day that had nothing to do with Grandfather Solomon, or my not knowing Hebrew, or feeling out of place.

Music. There was something in the melodies—I didn't need words—so foreign, and yet so familiar. I had arrived at the home I'd longed for, but didn't believe I would ever find.

My grandfather and I went to many Shabbat services together, and I got used to his off-key singing. He was praying, after all, if God didn't care, who was I to object? I just slumped in my seat, hummed along beside him, and let the music carry me away.

Grandfather Solomon died two years later, closing the chapter on my attending services. I missed going, but I wasn't brave enough to go alone. I decided that reading Holocaust literature and writing poetry could take the place of sitting in synagogue, hearing the ancient melodies.

But it didn't, and longing took up its familiar place in my heart. Yearning became such a part of my life that it felt normal. I stopped noticing it. Besides, I had other things that demanded my attention: college, graduate school, falling in love with Ruth. Missing a Jewish life receded into the background.

After Ruth and I had been together for ten years we decided to start a family. When I got pregnant, the realization grew, along with my unborn child, that some things would have to be different. Whoever this child turned out to be, he or she *would* have a Jewish life. This knowledge comforted to me as I eagerly anticipated the birth.

Ruth's mother, Gabbie, was the first to burst my bubble. When I was eight months pregnant, she came for a visit and, being helpful, offered to help me do dishes after dinner. As I leaned over my enormous belly, I attempted to steer the conversation toward safe topics—weather? travel plans?—when she interrupted, demanding, "What do you plan to do about this child's Jewish education?"

I knew the answer, but I hadn't expected to be asked. This soon, anyway. "Well, we'll take Noah—if it's a boy—and Sophie—if it's a girl—to synagogue, and when the kid is thirteen we'll have a bar or bat mitzvah." It was a mouthful, but it was true.

Staring intently at a spot just beyond my left ear, Gabbie spoke. "No synagogue in the world will consider you a family," she intoned. Truth declared.

When Noah was born, we gave him a Hebrew name, and when he was eight his Jewish education began. You remember that Ruth and I had separated just before he turned two and Noah spent most weekends with her. She lived too far away for him to go to religious school at our synagogue. So I found a tutor, a college boy majoring in Philosophy and Jewish Studies, and when it was time for Noah to be bar mitzvahed, he could chant effortlessly in biblical Hebrew.

That was when I had my first *aliyah*. Ruth and I had remained close, both intimately involved in Noah's life. As he studied, we planned for his bar mitzvah like it was the major event of the year. When our names were called, we walked to the *bimah* together, the first divorced lesbian parents in the synagogue ever to sing the blessing and wrap their thirteen-year-old in a *tallit*. We each gave a speech about what Noah meant to us, and we each cried.

My mother had died many years before, and by this time my father had converted. As a Quaker, he could not participate in Jewish rituals. Noah picked out a reading that he thought his grandpa would especially like. It was about peace, and my father read it, smiling at Noah the whole time.

That all happened five years earlier, so having had that experience, the congregation leaders undoubtedly considered themselves experts at handling the lesbian parent situation. Soon it would be Sophie's turn to become a bat mitzvah. As her parents, Anna and I were being honored with an *aliyah*. I knew I couldn't refuse, and I knew with equal certainty that I just could not sing the blessing, even though I'd done it before with Ruth. Somehow I couldn't sort out why it felt so different from the first time. So impossible.

I talked it over with Anna. "You're used to deferring," she said. "Usually you take a backseat, because you're a therapist trying to help people figure out what *they* think. Or you're Noah's or Sophie's mother. But this is you."

That was it. It would just be me singing, even though Anna would be standing there beside me, it would be my voice—me alone—singing the words.

My friend Eli understood. "An *aliyah*," he said simply, "is an experience well beyond what it seems to be."

I was stuck, so I invented a word game to distract myself. I called it "The Game of Emphasis."

I can't do it.
I **can't** do it.
I can't **do** it.
I can't do **it**.

Whatever way I repeated it to myself, it ended up meaning the same thing. I just knew I could not stand up there on Rosh Hashanah in front of all those people next to my spouse who happened to be a woman, and bless the Torah as if it were the most natural thing in the world for me. As if I belonged there.

Once I'd had my tantrum and exhausted myself with The Emphasis Game, it was obvious I would have to try something else. Accustomed to asking questions, I turned to myself: *What are you so afraid of? What's the worst that could happen?*

That was easy:

1. I'd blank out, opening my mouth to sing and nothing would come out.
2. I'd throw up.
3. I'd cry.

So those were the worst-case scenarios.

So I took stock. My tantrum hadn't gotten me anywhere. I'd fantasized the worst, which hadn't diminished my fear. There was just one week before Rosh Hashanah. So I did the only thing left. I started to learn the blessing.

I put the prayer book on the living room bookcase I walked by a hundred times a day. Every time I passed it, I picked up the book, and read the prayer. After a couple of days I started to sing it. Sometimes I'd belt it out like an opera singer, sometimes I'd sing it softly like a love song, or a lullaby. And when the week was over, I knew my *aliyah*.

I sang it to Noah and Sophie, who corrected my pronunciation, but eventually gave me a passing mark, "You sound okay." I sang it to Anna who smiled and didn't correct anything.

On Rosh Hashanah morning I made everyone get up early. When we arrived, we took our seats up front, which was easy, since only the rabbi and the president were there. Once the service started, I studied how the other couples receiving the blessing touched the Torah with their prayer book (women) or *tallit* (men) and kissed it, how they shook hands with the rabbi and the president afterwards.

Then our names were called, mine and Anna's. I do not remember how we got up there, but suddenly, there we were standing in front of everyone. The rabbi pointed to the verse on the scroll, I touched the Torah gently with my prayer book, took a breath and sang: "*Barchu et Adonai ham'vorach*." There it was, that ancient music coming out of my mouth, while I stood, Anna warm by my side, my grandfather singing softly in my ear (he was finally in tune), the little girl, Petra, whispering the words. The rabbi smiled as he shook my hand.

I remember every step of the walk back to my seat, wrapped in my own invisible *tallit*.

Happy New Year.

Sophie

27

The Dress

"But what will I *wear*?" Sophie's voice crescendoed into a wail. "We've only got four more months and we haven't even started to look."

Wear? We're talking about clothes now, when you barely know your haftorah? When you're still learning the trope?

But I exercised a modicum of self-control. I didn't say it. I did not point out that clothes are not the important thing, that this should be a spiritual experience, that family is coming, she is coming of age. No, I controlled myself, I did not lecture. I said, "I know it doesn't seem like very long, but I'm sure we have enough time to find something special. Do you want to go shopping tomorrow?"

"But where can we go? There's not one decent store in this stupid, hick town. We don't even have a mall."

Translation: Can you believe it?

Well, at least we agree on one thing—not that it's a hick town—but the fact is, we don't have a mall. Why in God's name do you think I moved us here anyway?

"We'll go shopping tomorrow morning. We'll start at Penney's and if we don't find anything we can go to TJ Maxx or Clays."

"Clays? You mean that store where everything is all natural fibers for old women?"

Hey, that's my favorite store you're talking about. That's where I got the great outfit for Noah's bar mitzvah, the purple pant suit with flowing pants that had an elastic waist. Very stylish.

"Okay, forget Clays. Where do you want to go?"

"There isn't anywhere," a sobbing shriek. We weren't "Just kidding, Mom" anymore; we were smack in the middle of a crisis.

How was I supposed to know? I've been worrying about finding a caterer, and whether she'd learn her parsha *in time. She's so lovely I never gave a second thought to what she would wear, I just knew it wouldn't be a problem finding an outfit that would set off her wavy auburn hair with blond highlights, and her soulful eyes.* Tears were streaming from those eyes now, catapulting me into a new reality. This was serious.

I jerked my head once—hard—trying to bring the present into sharp focus. Because instead of seeing her in the depth of despair, I was staring at another girl. Who looked surprisingly like her, but wasn't. Slimmer, sullen: I was looking at my seventeen-year-old self, shifting from leg to leg, in a just-bought prom dress. I wasn't in love with the boy I was going to the junior prom with, and I most definitely wasn't in love with the dress my mother told me I looked lovely in, talking around the pins in her mouth as she kneeled below me, folding the hem.

"No. Shorter!" Staring down at her bent head, noticing even more gray hair than that morning.

It was a terrible dress. Mustard yellow, some nubbly material. Not tulle, not velvet, not taffeta. Wrong color, wrong fabric. And sleeveless. My disgusting, hairy arms hung down, exposed. Why hadn't I bought the pale green thing? At least it had long sleeves. But, no, my mother said this fit better, and besides it cost half as much.

"I want to go to Burlington or Boston. And if I don't find anything then I have to go to New York. Rebecca's mother took her to the City and had a seamstress custom-make her dress."

But Rebecca's mother's from the City and knows how to find a seamstress there. "How about we look at the shops here tomorrow and if we don't find anything we'll make a plan?"

The Dress

Hiccupping between gulping sobs, she shrugged, heading towards her room, softly calling her dog. I wasn't invited.

By the next morning, we were friends again when I took her out to breakfast before starting our search. I'm a firm believer in not shopping on an empty stomach. In the first store, we established a routine: she'd choose whatever she wanted to try on, disappearing into the dressing room. When she was ready, her outstretched arm would emerge from the slightly opened door, summoning me, before banging shut. The voice imperious, through the slated doors: "Get this in a size 12" or "No way."

After a storeful of this, we'd come up empty-handed and set off for Store #2. Same result. By now, our relationship in jeopardy, by mutual agreement we decided to call it quits. I was about to concede her point about this being a bit of a hick town.

Life was back to normal by Monday, full of homework and Hebrew chanting, with no mention of the disastrous shopping expedition. The quest for the perfect dress seemed like ancient history. That is, until a week later when I arrived at the synagogue to pick her up. I spied her coming down the hall, looking sheepish as she sidled along in the shadow of her teacher, Rachel.

"Hi, sweetie, what's up? Is something wrong?"

"Oh, hi, Mom. No, it's just that . . ." Looking hopefully up at Rachel.

"Sophie asked me to take her shopping for her dress," Rachel filled in. "I was planning a shopping trip to Burlington this week, I'd be happy to take her."

On the way to the car, "Rachel's just so *cool*, she's got such great taste," Sophie gushed. "I'm sure we can find something. And then you don't have to go with me, Mom." Doing me a favor.

Is there a word for when you're devastated and relieved at the same time?

They went straight from school the next day, and Sophie didn't get home until 11:30. Groggy, she stumbled into the house, words slurred with fatigue. "Great time," she said, heading to her room. "Got a couple of things, but not *the* dress, and really the stores in Burlington aren't all they're cracked up to be." Collapsing into bed. "I'll show you tomorrow."

Rachel called the next morning to debrief. "She's impossibly picky," she said, trying not to whine. "Lots of things fit her, she looked really cute, but she found something wrong with everything. And she wouldn't let me make any suggestions. She got a couple of things, but I think she bought them to get me off her case."

Back to square one.

There was one more place we hadn't tried, Rosie Jekes, the only truly hip store in town. Sophie had suggested it, but I'd exercised veto power because the clothes are impossibly slinky, and expensive. Sophie hasn't had a growth spurt yet, she has a belly that's round and sweet, but the truth is she's really not svelte. Shopping in a store with all size 6's can be more than a little demoralizing. But it was Rosie Jekes, or I could envision New York looming in my future.

"I've changed my mind, honey. One more store. We'll just take a quick look, and if there isn't anything we'll come up with a plan." *I keep saying that, hoping something will spring to mind.*

The store is an old grange with all original architectural features preserved. New Hampshire version of restrained sophistication: scarred wood floors, gold-leaf letters announcing *Sundries* in fancy script, dressing rooms draped with faded, but still elegant, red velvet curtains.

Sophie went straight to a rack of dresses, flipping purposefully along the row.

No point in my picking out anything. I'll just stand here and wait.

"Hey, Mom, look at this."

The dress she's holding up is black, some shimmery material, hopelessly narrow.

"Do you think it'll fit?"

I stand outside the dressing room, already anticipating the disappointment that will cloud her face.

It's not my thirteen-year-old Sophie who emerges, brushing aside the velvet curtain. It's some other woman: a flamenco dancer in a tight black gown that hugs her hips, swaying to show off an insert of blood-red at the scalloped hem. Shoulders back, head high, the dancer twirls in slow circles, bare feet stepping a grapevine to her own music across the worn wood floor.

"Mom, it's *me,*" as she starts chanting her Haftorah softly to herself.

28

On the Bridge, Twice

OICE 1

Oh, no, I'm going to see her there today. It's always like this on Thursday mornings. Why do I have to pass right by her? She'll be standing there, expecting me to wave like everything's normal. Which it most certainly is not, because I'm sitting in the front seat next to Noah who's driving and muttering, "Goddamnit, why's she have to go every week?" and he won't honk even though I remind him she says we have to.

She'll be holding one of the signs that sits in our hall the rest of the week, waiting. What'll it be today? WAR ISN'T HEALTHY FOR CHILDREN, maybe. Or, STOP THE WAR NOW, BRING THE BOYS HOME! even though I've told her that's sexist, and women are soldiers now, too.

At least she's not as bad as the guy with the long gray ponytail who stands on a different corner in the main part of town. He's there every week, too. I know his kids, and boy, are they messed up. But there's one thing I've got to say to her and I can promise you it's not going to be easy. But I've got to do it—"Mom, lose the hat." I don't care that it's been ten below every Thursday for the past month. This is important. Get some new headgear.

I know everything she's going to say back to me: Clothes are trivial. War is wrong. It's important to stand up for what you believe in. Dissent is patriotic. Yeah, yeah. But why does she have to stand up for what she believes in where all my friends can see her?

I know all about the people in towns just like ours who are trying to go about their daily lives while we drop bombs on them. I know about the old people and babies in their mothers' arms crouching in basements trembling and praying.

Before she left this morning she asked me if I'd go with her to stand on the bridge next week and I told her I didn't know. She said, "It's important for young people to be out there, too." I know, I know, but Mom, I've got a big French test next Thursday and you remember you told me to bring my average up? Well, I'm trying.

VOICE 2

Damn it, where's my hat? rummaging through the scarves, gloves and caps in the antique apple crate that holds winter clothes. *It's been so cold standing on the bridge with the wind whipping off the river, I'll need the warmest hat I can find, the red boiled wool one. The kids hate it, but who cares? I know it's shabby and faded and that I got it at my favorite used clothes store, but it's me out there with cold ears if I don't wear it. That's the one I need because it has ear flaps.*

Walking down the hill, hat found, pushed back at a jaunty angle—for an instant it feels like all's right with the world, even though it's not even 7:00 in the morning. *Except all the things that aren't right, starting with this war.* Still, there's something gratifying about going to a vigil, something so familiar. So old. *It's because I'm a child of the 60's,* I remind myself, as I turn the corner and see a scattering of other middle-aged people, mostly gray-haired women, holding signs. All of us aging hippies, that's what we are. *All we are saying is give peace a chance.*

A blast of icy wind jolts me, carrying with it an ancient memory. Not of being younger like during the '60s, but of being *young*.

I'm five. I'm with my mommy and daddy and my big brother, Benny. We're in a small crowd of people, milling around in front of the state capital. I can't see much besides legs, except when my dad picks me up so I can look over the people's heads. That's when I see them, the men in suits. They're standing close together in groups on the steps that go up to the big building. They all seem to be wearing the same dark suit, and there's something about how they stand with one hand on their hips, tugging down their jackets. As Daddy lowers me down I'm confused about what I think I saw. That can't be right. It looked like a gun was poking out from behind the suit jackets. I look up to Mommy. "Who are those men?" and she tells me, "Those men are our legislators, they run our state."

Mommy and Daddy say, "Come on, we're leaving," as we move to the edge of the crowd. Mommy holds my hand tight, *Ow, she's hurting me!* and she's got Benny with her other hand. There's a lot of noise and then all of a sudden, out of nowhere, a young guy in a T-shirt and jeans runs up, yelling at my dad. He's screaming at the top of his lungs, using bad words, "What the hell do you think you're doing, you Nigger-lover?" Getting right up close into Daddy's face. Daddy looks confused, like he doesn't know what to do. Just when I think the guy's going to sock him, Daddy puts his sign down on the ground and sits on it. The young guy dances around him, screaming and kicking the pavement. "Get up, you yellow-bellied Nigger-lover! You Christ-killer! Get up and fight like a man!" But Daddy just sits there looking up at him, smiling his half-smile.

That's the memory the icy wind delivered. Before I ever heard of Martin Luther King or civil disobedience I saw my own father sit down in protest.

 VOICE 1

You know what I haven't told her? It's about my dreams. I've been dreaming about babies, lots of babies. Maybe it's because my cousin Leni just had hers last week. Sometimes it's Leni's new baby I dream about—they named her Gemma, for my grandma who died before I was born—but sometimes it's other infants in their mothers' arms hiding in those basements. They're always crying and their mothers are cooing softly, trying to comfort them.

Okay. Okay. I'll go with her. But I've got to get up my courage to tell her what's been on my mind. I hope to God she'll listen.

"Mom, I'll come stand on the bridge with you, but you've got to do this one thing for me. If it's still cold out, please, please promise me you'll wear a different hat."

Noah

29

Hiking

I'M FINE, I TOLD myself. *I'll just lie here and catch my breath. I can just stay right where I am. In fact, maybe I'll stay here forever.*

I lie on the ground beneath the big rock I'd slipped off trying to figure out how badly I was hurt. My companion's back had disappeared a long time ago. I'd been following his dark green pack that blended in with the scrub trees and rocks, with a jaunty splash of purple and orange that had encouraged me: *Come along, you can do it*. And I had, until now.

Now I was down, and the back was gone.

But I'm starting in the middle. Let me tell you the whole story about how I got myself into this mess.

"I've decided this is an absurd activity," Noah called to me at the beginning of our hike the day before. Staring at his huge backpack, I was trying not to add to his grumpiness by agreeing. Our first 3.8 miles stretched before us—mostly uphill—and we were getting a late start. But what was the point of hating every step? Then again, there was something to ponder here. He went on, interrupting my private questioning, *What* is *the point*?

"I've been thinking about it. What's the point of leaving my room where I have everything I need, taking it all, plus food and a tent, putting it on my back and carrying it all uphill?" His voice practically cracking at the final outrage, *uphill*. "For miles?"

That question lingered as we set off. A steep climb. Up. The things you learn on the trail are primary: the reds and blues and yellows of hiking. After fifteen minutes I remembered them from years I've done this before: watch where you step, it's hard going up, but it hurts even more coming down. I understand with renewed appreciation where the cliché "the rocky road" comes from as I stumble on yet another stone in my path. I treasure the occasional flat sections where you walk on soft leaves and pine needles. I breathe gratitude then. When we're climbing I use my hiking mantra to set the rhythm: *one foot in front of the other, one foot in front of the other.*

Then there are the signs. They appear unexpectedly, providing a relief from the beauty that quickly becomes monotonous: rock, root, and tree. Small, white block print on green background, they announce the important things: VIEW, WATER, SHELTER. Of course, there are the trail blazes, and the weathered signs that tell you how much farther to your destination. Sometimes I make Noah stand in front of one so I can document where we've been, and where we're going. He gazes out at me, disgruntled at having his picture taken, squinting into the sun.

And then, like a surprise guest, there's one of the signs. VIEW. Noah's nowhere to be seen so I head down the detour alone, and find him, sitting out on the edge of a rock ledge, admiring the vista. I pause quietly to admire him sitting out there, knowing I'd never do it, before I announce myself. "Hey."

"Hey," he says, "look at this view. It was all worth it."

I drop my pack and join him, standing with my back against the rock face. We can see the hut we came from far below, and look straight across to the summit of Wildcat Mountain. The view made even more marvelous with the pride of ownership. For now, it's *our* view. We earned it.

On.

Next time we stop we're on the summit of Mt. Hight, one of the 4000-footers, as they're called. I don't really care, although there are people who do, keeping lists of all the mountains they've summited. *Like people who keep lists of birds. I don't understand this mania for lists.* I just want to stand there above tree line and know I've climbed up there myself, to feel what it's like not to have anything higher than I am. I have a short person's sensitivities; every once in a while I need to be the tallest. There's a young couple climbing up behind us, tan, shiny with health and energy. I interrupt their conversation. "Hey, would you mind taking our picture right here by the summit sign?" and seizing the opportunity, just so nothing *will* be towering over me, I climb onto the rocks, making my head even with Noah's. They nod, smile, the guy takes my camera and then, click, the photo's taken. To make conversation I ask them how long they've been on the trail.

"Since March," the young man says, "five months."

"Wow. That's a long time. And you're still talking to each other?"

He gazes at her, radiant, like a dazzling shaft of sun illuminating the air between them. "Oh, *absolutely.*" I've only seen that look on one other person's face, Anna gazing at me when I'm telling her something I've never told anyone before. *God, I wish she were here just to see this view.* The young couple shoulders their packs and stride off, leaving me with the slightly sour taste of having asked that question.

Next summit, next young couple, smiling, talking. Noah's teasing me about how slow I am, after he's hiked twenty minutes he has to stop and wait ten for me to catch up. Which means I never get a good rest, because he's ready to go when I finally arrive. We step aside, good trail etiquette, for the faster couple to pass. I say to them, "He's making fun of how slow I go," really just kidding. The young woman pauses, looking Noah straight in the eye. "Each person can only go at their own pace," she says, heading down the trail. Her partner follows close behind. "She has to wait for me on the uphills," he adds, while she calls back, "and he's faster going down." They pass by, their message hovering behind them.

But I guess I wasn't really heeding their message. I understood it, it was as obvious as the trail signs—GO AT YOUR OWN

PACE— but it's hard to resist the urge to hurry. We'd already been walking for a couple of hours and I was starting to get shaky. Usually I stop to drink water, or eat some gorp when this happens, but I was trying to catch up with Noah so he wouldn't have to wait so long. And that's when I fell. I caught my toe, my pack unweighted me and I slid down a long face of rock, landing on my knees and side of my face on the hard-packed trail. Shrugging off my pack, untangling my legs, I lay there, feeling all the parts that hurt. *Geez, at least nothing's bleeding or broken. At least I don't think so.*

I got up, first on all fours, then, slowly standing. I retrieved the pack, *at least I was alone, no one witnessed that long slide off the rock. My pride is what hurts the most. Time to listen to what people tell you on the trail: go at your own pace.*

That's when the conversations started. First, it was the quads: "How could you ask us to do this for so long? Don't you know anything about preparing for a long hike? What kind of a moron are you, anyway?"

Then the collarbones chimed in: "Yeah, and how about more padding up here. The rest of you is padded enough obviously, but we're sticking out here taking all the weight." And far off in the distance, a whimper I could barely make out. The feet: "Don't pay any attention to them. We're the ones taking all the weight here." Then they started to argue among themselves: "And why did you stupid middle toes get band aids, don't we deserve band aids, too? No, make that moleskin!" Those were the big toes. Louder whimpers: "We'll make you pay for this."

Who knew body parts could talk?

So it was me and my complaining body that made it down the trail to the next stop where Noah was waiting. I mentioned my fall like it was a minor mishap, deciding to keep my arguing body parts to myself. We drank some water, and headed off again.

There were so many other people on the trail it didn't feel like solitary communing with Mother Nature like it had in previous years. In fact, it was starting to feel like a Pirandello play or an outdoor circus. The next characters certainly added color. They were Jack #1, skinny and frenetic, and Jack #2, stolid and sincere. The first Jack tried to engage Noah in a discussion of his plans for next year. "Are you graduating next year? Where do you want to go to school? What do you plan to study?"—peppering him with questions. Noah was reluctant to reveal anything personal, out of habit or embarrassment, hard to tell. Then, the comment that unlocked the gate: Jack #1: "So it's not like you know you want to be an electrical engineer or something like that?" Which is *exactly* what Noah thinks he wants to be, and said so. That was all the response Jack #1 needed. He started to extol the virtues of MIT, his alma mater, and described his meteoric career path. He asked Noah's SAT scores, and allowed as how they weren't half bad, adding, "I got six 800's and one 795." This thirty-five years after the fact. Still smarting from that 795, apparently.

To change the subject, I told the Jacks how hard the downhills were on my knees. I didn't mention that they'd been screaming at me and calling me rude names. How was I supposed to know that this provided the perfect introduction to the topic of correct downhill walking? Jack #2 gave the lecture while Jack #1 provided the demonstration by prancing, leaping nimbly from rock to rock. Which was impressive since he wasn't even wearing hiking boots, only Tevas and socks. The dialogue that accompanied it was succinct, though confusing: "Walk on your balls, walk on your balls," they chanted in unison. I turned to Jack #2. "He's been out here too long," gesturing towards Jack #1. And Jack #1, not missing a beat, chimed in, "I've been out for thirty years." That's when I noticed Noah staring at the rainbow flag sewn on Jack's baseball cap. He nodded knowingly, as we walked off down the trail.

Noah and I laughed. "He just likes to hear himself say 'balls,'" he whispered confidentially. We shook our heads and admonished each other whenever our conversation slowed, "Walk on your balls." Which is what I was trying to do once he'd left me alone again to find my own pace. I thought I'd found a pretty good rhythm, hitting my stride for the next hour or so. Then in the distance I spied a beautiful bright yellow canopy. *What's this? Some* kind of a tarp? *Maybe Noah's found a place to rest and we can set up camp early. Maybe there are people there who'd like to carry my pack for me for a while*—as I got closer, closer.

Then I could distinguish what it was. Fall comes early in these mountains. The brilliant gold of poplar leaves arching over the trail created a stunning, impressive display, one that had nothing to do with tarps or stopping.

Who knew how much longer—I was so tired I lost track of time—there was the sign for the cut-off to the shelter. I couldn't remember how long this new trail was. Stumbling. Resting. Calling out, "Noah, Noah!" He was so far ahead, he never heard.

Then, there he was, coming *towards* me. I was so used to following his back I didn't know what to think. *Is he okay, is he falling down with exhaustion too? What would we do then?* But no, he didn't look exhausted and he wasn't carrying his pack.

"Here, Mom, let me take that for you." He reached for my pack.

I just leaned against a rock, whimpering. "How much farther is it?"

"Half a mile. Look, I'll carry it." Slinging my pack over his shoulder, and heading off. This time I followed his back with my smaller pack, *this is much farther than half a mile.*

"I thought you said it was half a mile."

A small smile, acknowledgement. "A slight distortion. I thought you needed some encouragement." Dropping my pack to the ground.

I didn't even care about eating. A cup of tea would do. All I wanted was my sleeping bag. But there was one final character to meet before sleep, Jason, calling himself J, the shelter caretaker. He came to collect the fee and chat after Noah had made us freeze-dried beans and rice for dinner. All I could think about was lying down, but J had some information about wilderness camping he was determined to communicate: please don't pee in the privy, peeing on the trail was best even though that didn't afford much privacy. Everything was composted, and it was easier if the poo was dry. He added, seriously, "I know. I work with the poo," offering to tell us more if we wanted. We looked at him, glanced at each other, and declined, silently shaking our heads. *No, that's okay, we get it.* But I could tell we had a new line to use if things got rough. "I know. I work with the poo."

It was barely dusk when J left, but I crawled into my sleeping bag, anyway. At last. I lay there remembering when Noah was a little boy, how I'd taken him on these hikes since he was eight years old, fortifying him with handfuls of M and M's for those long uphill climbs. This was our ninth year hiking together. Now he had stubble after one day on the trail and my knees complained after just a couple of hours. But we still tell each other jokes and we still meet characters on our path and we're still out in the mountains together.

Noah, Noah, I've got it, resisting sleep. *That's the point.* I turned over to tell him, but he was sprawled out on the ground next to me, dead asleep.

30

Dear John

EAR JOHN,

I don't have enough words, or the right words, to express the gratitude I feel towards you. Although we've never met and maybe never will, your donation nineteen years ago was the gift of life. The result of that gift, my son Noah, has been a joy and a blessing. When he received the manila envelope yesterday he said quietly, "Look, information about my father," as he opened it, and there was your photograph along with ones of your sister, mother, and father. Thanks for including those: they give a picture of his history that no one else could provide.

Noah has missed knowing you, but I don't think he's suffered. Ruth and I separated when he was a toddler, but we've both stayed actively—he might say *too* actively—involved in his life.

I told him where he came from one day when he was about four-years-old, and I was going to donate blood. We were standing in the line together when I had a flash—one of those things you realize that's so obvious you can't imagine you never thought of it before—that donating blood and semen are both gifts of life. I told Noah about you that day. I told him that we knew his father was a good man because he made a special kind of donation.

He's talked about you at various times in his life. Once he understood that his family was "different," he asked about who you were and I passed along what I knew. I wrote down some of those conversations so I wouldn't forget. Here's one:

> When can I meet my daddy?
> When you're eighteen.
> How do you know that?
> Because he said when you're eighteen if you want to meet him, he wants to meet you.
> How did you talk to him?
> I didn't talk to him but I talked to someone who knows him and that's what he said.
> Why when I'm eighteen, why not fourteen?
> What's better about fourteen?
> It's closer to four.

So you see, John, you've been on Noah's mind for a long time.

He's often wondered about where his interest and ability in math and science comes from since these aren't my strengths. He likes to tease me about this, and he credits my father who's a scientist. And he credits you. He knows you're an electrical engineer. Who knows how much that has to do with his idea that he wants to be one. Anyway, when it was time to think about colleges he decided to apply to MIT, even though he didn't think he'd get in. "Anyone who wants to be an engineer *has* to apply to MIT," he said. I told him I admired his willingness to take the risk, and then, much to our mutual surprise, he was accepted. So off he goes in the fall, and we'll see what direction his interests and abilities take him.

He wrote his college essay about meeting you. I hope if he decides to write you directly he'll send you a copy. It's a beautiful piece that made me cry, partly for his yearning and partly for his appreciation of his life, and for Ruth and me as his parents. And you'll see that he understands in the deepest possible way what being a sperm donor means to a family.

John, you have my undying appreciation. I hope that your life is good, that you and your family are well and happy, and that you ride many miles on your bike in good health.

I guess I should add that Noah has become an avid bicyclist. When he learned about your passion for bike touring, he smiled and said, "I think I'll go for a long ride."

With lifelong gratitude,
Jesse

Love Made Visible

31

Characters

WELL, YOU'VE HEARD ABOUT my falling in love with Anna, and about Sophie and Noah growing up, leaving gaping holes in my life that were begging to be filled. The search for my dropped stitches was paying off, I felt more centered and whole than ever before. Retirement had provided the luxury of time to reflect, writing was challenging, but would it be enough?

So it was back to looking for part-time work. As you know, it'd been hard for me to figure out what, if anything, I wanted to do, besides write these stories. I was either overqualified:

DELIVERY DRIVER—must have clean driver's license

or underqualified:

PROFESSOR OF CLINICAL PSYCHOLOGY, PHD required

or simply not qualified:

WAREHOUSE WORKER, must be able to lift 75 lbs easily

or,

GARAGE DOOR TECH, installing and repairing garage doors and openers, top pay for experience.

So, despairing of finding anything, I'd mostly stopped looking seriously.

But last year, due to ever-increasing free time as Noah departed for college and Sophie needed less of me, I'd started looking again, and as I flipped through the paper, randomly scanning the ads, there it was—the perfect job. Not a job really, more like a job-*chik*.

> UNIVERSITY MEDICAL SCHOOL: seeking M/F 30–50 years to role play as patients for medical student education. Afternoon hours, training and compensation provided.

It had everything: prestige (University Medical School), teaching (medical student education), drama (role playing). It was part-time. So I was fifty-three, I was sure I could look fifty. They probably just meant middle-aged: somewhat overweight, slightly deaf, gray hair. *That's me you're talking about. I'm versatile, I can play any character you want. I'm the perfect candidate.*

I sent off my resume with a cover letter, adding facts that weren't immediately obvious: I had been a drama major my first year in college, I'd recently been ill and knew about medical care from a patient's perspective.

Hire me!

While I was waiting to be called for an interview, something kept niggling, trying to reach up into my consciousness.

It was my mother. When she was fifty-three she had her breast amputated. She wrote an article about it for a nursing journal and when her surgeon asked for her help making an educational film for surgical residents, she readily agreed. She loved being interviewed, answering questions the doctor asked, even lifting her blouse to show her scar. It gave her a chance to speak her mind, to tell young surgeons what they should and shouldn't say to patients. She told this story:

> I was seen for a follow-up visit by Dr. ____, a surgical resident. He asked me if I wore my prosthesis and I told him I didn't; it just wasn't comfortable. When he asked what I did instead I told him I wore my husband's T-shirts. The young doctor paused and said, "Oh, Mrs. Silverman, don't do that to your husband." I thought, *It's okay, I can buy*

him more T-shirts. That seemed an easy solution, until I realized what he meant.

She looked straight into the camera then: "Don't ever say that to a woman."

They called yesterday and I went for the interview. I went as a middle-aged woman; gray hair, sagging breasts. I didn't mention that my mother came too, and sat silently by my side.

I got hired on the spot. I was exactly who they were looking for. They didn't offer my mother anything, but that was okay. She just winked at me, smiling in that way she had that made you feel like the most important person in the world.

That's us, characters together.

32

Thanks to Itzhak

ANNA'S BIRTHDAY WAS COMING up in just three months and I set out on a mission. I was on the trail of the perfect present, something she would really treasure. It's not every day that you turn sixty after all. But there were major stumbling blocks: she didn't need anything and, as far as I could tell, she didn't *want* anything, either. Plus she was always making comments about how she chooses gifts—bread or candles or flowers—that "don't leave anything behind to deal with." Obviously she didn't want more *things*. So the mission promised to be a challenging one.

Until I noticed the ad in the college paper for a concert of classical music, Tchaikovsky's Violin Concerto, Opus 35, I knew I was looking at it, THE gift. Now, I don't know anything about classical music, but Anna does. When she was growing up they were only permitted to listen to the Masters: Beethoven, Brahms, Tchaikovsky. While someone else (say, me) might have resented such rigid control of musical taste, Anna fell in love with violin, cello, and orchestra. She still listens to Brahms to soothe herself. "It's in my blood," she tells me, when I suggest the blues or Joan Baez. "Neurological memory."

But back to the perfect gift: that concert ticket. I arrived at the ticket booth an hour before tickets went on sale, just in case, joining a crowd of polite, eager classical music aficionados. Feeling entirely out of place—like a fraud in the house of culture—I figured if I kept my mouth shut no one would know. I'd pocket my tickets and leave, anticipating Anna's face when she opened the birthday card, and a ticket (or two, if I got lucky) fell out.

When the time came, our crowd formed itself into a tidy line, walked one-by-one to the window, only to turn away, dejected. No one seemed mad, just perplexed. Word filtered back: no tickets available to the general public. Seems all seats had been bought in advance by an elite cadre, The Friends of the College. Leaving nothing for those of us less "friendly."

Hopes dashed, I started in on a silent litany of complaints: *How could they advertise tickets and not save any for the public? Who were these Friends anyway? No friend of mine.*

I joined the trickle of rejected concert-goers, wandering away.

Normally, I would have told Anna this story, embellishing to make it even more preposterous. But I couldn't. I had to sequester it, until I could figure out what to do. It marinated inside, becoming a fine stew of longing and outrage.

After a couple of days spent stirring the stew, a new possibility occurred to me. The time-honored approach of the un-ticketed of the world. Scalping.

But have I mentioned who was playing?

Itzhak Perlman. Even I knew the name. Who was going to sell their ticket to an Itzhak Perlman concert? And who would have enough money to *buy* a ticket if anyone would part with one?

Scalping was impossible.

Still, I had to try. I made signs with those little tear-off strips with my phone number. I worked to strike the right note between urgent need and musical desire.

> DESPERATELY NEED 1 OR 2 TICKETS!
> TO ITZHAK PERLMAN CONCERT.
> SPECIAL BIRTHDAY GIFT.
> WILL PAY.

You bet, I'll pay, I thought as I tacked up the signs in the obvious places: two food co-ops, one yoga studio, three campus events boards.

I waited. Of course, no one called. *I'll wait a couple more days before I give up and go look for the second-most-perfect birthday present. Whatever that might be.*

Finally, resigned, I went shopping. I didn't hold out much hope since, as you already know, our small college town is not a shopping mecca. It's not that there aren't stores, it's just that they're so *preppy*. After a brief foray, I returned home empty-handed to a message on my answering machine. "Hello" a lightly-accented woman's voice began, "I saw your sign for tickets. You can call me at home," leaving the number. I dialed, immediately. The ticket-seller gave me directions, she'd be there for an hour or so, could I come over?

Could I come over? I'm there. I jumped in the car, and drove the fifteen minutes to her house, knocked, and who should answer but Alice Obermeyer, a doctor I vaguely knew from when I'd worked at the hospital. We hadn't recognized each other's voice, and here we were staring at each other through the open door.

"Oh, it's you, Jesse," she said. "Come in, would you like some tea?" Now, I don't really drink tea, but I wasn't going to jeopardize the possibility of scoring the tickets. "Sure." I nodded as we sat down at her kitchen table.

"What have you been doing since you left the hospital?" Alice inquired. I filled her in on my retirement, my writing, trying to see as much of Noah as he'd allow during his last year at home.

Alice had a high school senior too; she nodded sympathetically. She was still working at the hospital, seeing patients, had just started a statewide program for families with kids who had chronic illnesses. "Hey," she said, thinking out loud. "Do you want a job?" Then, realizing what she'd just said, she tried to backpedal, having just offered something she didn't have. "The woman who's the program manager doesn't seem to like the job. If she leaves, would you be interested?"

Interested? Maybe. "I'm in the enviable position of not *having* to work, not yet anyway. I only want to work at something that's challenging and that I care about. But fill me in."

She did. We chatted a bit longer; she gave me the two tickets—I'd get to go after all—and I handed over a lot of money. Alice kept one ticket for herself. She'd share Anna's birthday concert with us.

I had to keep this secret for the week until Anna's birthday, which wasn't easy, I was so proud of having scored the tickets. During the birthday dinner I kept my mouth shut through the main course, holding on till dessert and coffee, which is when I'd decided to give her the card. As anyone who knows Anna will tell you, she loves surprises and her enthusiasms are boundless.

As she opened the card, I struggled to maintain my equilibrium, while she carefully examined the antique photograph on the front, commenting on the unique combination of color and shadow—*wait,* I'm thinking, *there's more!*—as the tickets dropped out onto the table. At first she barely glanced at them, reading the note inside. Then she picked one up, stared blankly at it, then—her face white—leapt to her feet and yelled, "Itzhak Perlman? Tchaikovsky's Violin Concerto? Where did you get these? Are they for me?" so loud that the other diners looked up from their conversations to smile at the sixty-year-old woman dancing around the table, waving tickets over her head.

The concert was extraordinary, although, I'm embarrassed to admit, I nodded off a couple of times, but Anna didn't notice. She was riveted. It was simply the best gift.

I was still applauding my gift-giving prowess the week after the concert, but then life returned to normal. Regular days, not birthdays: struggling with my writing, alternating between anticipating and dreading Noah's departure.

Sophie had her bat mitzvah, and turned into the full-fledged teenager we'd caught glimpses of for the past year. In mid-August we took Noah to college. Back to being at home with my teenager, my writing, volunteer work, and wondering how else to fill my time.

Then just last week, a full two years after the Itzhak Perlman concert, I returned home from an emergency meeting in New York. The family business was floundering, and our entire family had gathered to debate the future of the company Grandpa Sam had started so many years before. As we talked our way around the table, each shareholder spoke of their emotional attachment to the company and their financial realities. I acknowledged that the business had funded my early retirement, and publicly thanked those family members whose work had made my new life possible. Everyone listened respectfully, but after the meeting my Uncle Herman pulled me close, hissing his hot breath into my good ear, "Get a job!"

What, my twenty-eight years as a therapist don't add up to anything? But his words were still stinging in my ears when I arrived back home and picked up my phone messages.

"Hello, Jesse." A vaguely familiar voice. It was Alice. "Remember when we talked two years ago? Well, if you're interested I have a job for you. Call me back."

I did, and at eight o'clock the next morning I met with Alice and her colleagues. The job of program manager was mine if I wanted it.

My job*chik* as a role-player was long over by the time my new job found me. I never thought I would work again, for money, anyway. Writing, volunteering, sure. But a real job that would require me to hear? *Good thing I finally got that hearing aid. Just in time.*

It's an interim position, that's true, so there's no guarantee how long I'll be employed. But it's exciting work. Young Benjamin's message rang in my ears: Care about the world. Be passionate, Do good work.

Retirement taught me a lot. But my days will be different now. Tomorrow morning I'll get up, put on something other than my sweat clothes, and go to work. Thanks to Itzhak.

33

Chinese Box

WHICH BRINGS US TO today.
The mammogram results were inconclusive—they want to see me again—so here I am again, with time between meetings with doctors. Should I sit in the designated area, wait hours until my next appointment when a total stranger will inform me of my future, following my mother's footsteps or another year of reprieve?

No. I need air. I walk down the endless hall toward the doors that, sensing my presence, open automatically to the outside. I start briskly down the block as if I'm heading somewhere important. But really I'm wandering, filling time, before my future.

Two blocks down, a destination appears: a craft fair, in full holiday swing. I glance at the first table, which barely slows me down; it's the second table that stops me dead. It's covered with boxes. Tall rectangular boxes, tiny boxes, boxes nesting in boxes. My eyes rove from one to the other, admiring each. It's not till I see a tall oblong in the deepest purple, shot through with threads of midnight blue, that I stop looking. The tall box covered in raw silk holds me, begging to be touched. But I'm not sure if I should, maybe it's just for looking.

The box is so beautiful that it hurts. I make myself turn away, delaying the pleasure of staring or, maybe, touching. I walk away, disciplining myself to stop at every other booth, nodding to the artists, pretending to admire hand-loomed scarves, hand-thrown pottery, silver jewelry, knowing I had fallen in love.

The box is there waiting for me after I finish my rounds. I stand gazing, indulging in that silent pleasure, and then tentatively reach out my hand to touch it.

"Beautiful, isn't it?" A lilting, musical voice stops me, mid-reach. I hadn't even seen the woman sitting behind the table. The box maker? And, embarrassed by my passionate attention to a box, I turn to her.

I recognize her. It is Zee, a woman who I know only by her story. Her son died in a climbing accident two years ago, just the age Noah is now. I've wanted to say something to her these past years, but you know how you talk yourself out of things? All the excuses we use so we don't have to talk about the hardest things: I *don't really know her*, and, *how do you speak the unspeakable, anyway?* and *maybe she doesn't want to be reminded* (as if your son's death is something you would forget). All the lies we tell ourselves.

"Zee, these are amazing. But this one—" reaching toward it again. She nods, a spark lighting her face as she stares at me gazing at her creation. In that fleeting moment you can imagine who she was before her boy fell, away from her. Forever.

"Yes, that one's special. But, look, there's more. Take off the top."

Permission to touch. I delicately lift the fitted lid and, in one fluid motion, the sides drop down flat on the table top, exposing a blood-red interior. Each panel separate, distinct, its own reality. Box no more.

And after the *more* Zee offered, there is more yet again. Each panel is filled with tools: needles, a rainbow of thread, miniature scissors, a silver thimble. It is a Chinese sewing box.

Without warning, I'm somewhere else, in another time, staring at the framed print that hangs in the front hall of my mother's house. Red calligraphy on a deep purple background, her favorite saying, WORK IS LOVE MADE VISIBLE.

I know the box is meant for me. I want to *be* that box. Capped closed when need be, but when the top is lifted, flat open, no hidden pockets, no secret drawers. Work to do. Tools to do it with. Love made visible.

The End

Afterword

Just a Dropped Stitch is a fictionalized memoir. By this I mean that the essence of the story is true although some of the facts and names have been changed. It is a story—a lifetime of stories—written entirely from my point of view.

While the facts of each person's life are unique, I hope that the stories of the dropped stitches and redeemed threads of Jesse's life will resonate with other daughters and sons, other mothers and fathers.

—L. L.

www.ingramcontent.com/pod-product-compliance
Lightning Source LLC
Chambersburg PA
CBHW070313230426
43663CB00011B/2111